POLICY AND PRACTIC

NUMBER THIRTEEN

INTER-AGENCY COLLABORATION: PROVIDING FOR CHILDREN

POLICY AND PRACTICE IN EDUCATION

1: Lindsay Paterson, *Education and the Scottish Parliament*

2: Gordon Kirk, *Enhancing Quality in Teacher Education*

3: Nigel Grant, *Multicultural Education in Scotland*

4: Lyn Tett, *Community Education, Lifelong Learning and Social Inclusion*

5: Sheila Riddell, *Special Educational Needs*

6: J. Eric Wilkinson, *Early Childhood Education: The New Agenda*

7: Henry Maitles, *Values in Education: We're All Citizens Now*

8: Willis Pickard and John Dobie, *The Political Context of Education after Devolution*

9: Jim O'Brien, Daniel Murphy and Janet Draper, *School Leadership*

10: Margaret Nicolson and Matthew MacIver (eds), *Gaelic Medium Education*

11: Gordon Kirk, Walter Beveridge and Iain Smith, *The Chartered Teacher*

12: Jim O'Brien, *The Social Agenda of the School*

13: Ann Glaister and Bob Glaister (eds), *Inter-Agency Collaboration: Providing for Children*

14: Mary Simpson and David Raffe, *Assessment*

POLICY AND PRACTICE IN EDUCATION

EDITORS

JIM O'BRIEN *AND* CHRISTINE FORDE

INTER-AGENCY COLLABORATION: PROVIDING FOR CHILDREN

Edited by

Ann Glaister and Bob Glaister
Formerly of the Open University

DUNEDIN ACADEMIC PRESS

EDINBURGH

Published by
Dunedin Academic Press Ltd
Hudson House
8 Albany Street
Edinburgh EH1 3QB
Scotland

ISBN 1 903765 14 5
ISSN 1479-6910

British Library Cataloguing in Publication Data
A catalogue record for this book is available from the British Library

Typeset by Patty Rennie Production, Portsoy
Printed in Great Britain by Cromwell Press

CONTENTS

Editorial Introduction   vi

Editors and Contributors   viii

Introduction: *Ann Glaister and Bob Glaister*   x

Chapter 1:   Inter-agency collaboration in context: 1
the 'joining-up' agenda, *Bronwen Cohen*

Chapter 2:   A model for educational change in   13
East Renfrewshire, *Jeannie Mackenzie*

Chapter 3:   Joint working in South Ayrshire Early Years Forum   25
Douglas Hutchison

Chapter 4:   Widening opportunities for disabled children in   36
Stirling: a voluntary body initiative, *Sue Dumbleton*

Chapter 5:   Developing integrated mental health services for   47
children and young people in Moray, *Chris Wiles*

Chapter 6:   Space for growth, *Ann Glaister and Bob Glaister*   58

Bibliography   73

Index   77

EDITORIAL INTRODUCTION

Ann and Bob Glaister have edited this new volume on inter-agency collaboration in the Policy and Practice in Education series. The editors are well placed to produce this volume through their long experience in teaching and research in education and health and social care at the Open University.

The Scottish Executive has stressed the need for 'joined up thinking and action' to be prioritised in relation to children's services and a series of initiatives and legal requirements now exist. Recognising and confirming that such policy development requires public services to transcend traditional demarcation lines and professional boundaries, the editors have brought together several authors who have expertise and experience in policy development and 'delivery'. Contributors include key managers and strategists from Children's Services, educational psychology, integrated community schools, clinical psychology and health and social care. They offer a grounded and theoretical perspective on the nature of inter-agency collaboration in the new devolved Scotland through a series of case studies.

The case studies and associated commentary and discussion provide an outline of policy development with appropriate illustration from across the range of initiatives and activities underway. The editors in the final chapter draw together some of the implications of inter-agency collaboration in practice and discuss the issues emerging in common from the case studies and what can be learned. Among the issues raised are those associated with the synergy between local development and how it relates to national policy; trust and communication between different professions; and the evolution of community-based partnerships with parents and young people and what these might mean for the contributing professionals. Policy-makers and practitioners will find much to consider in the case studies and discussion which point a way forward in a number of challenging ways.

Dr Jim O'Brien
Vice Dean and Director, Centre for
Educational Leadership, Faculty of
Education, Moray House School of
Education, The University of Edinburgh

Dr Christine Forde
Senior Lecturer
in Educational Studies
The University of Glasgow

EDITORS AND CONTRIBUTORS

Bronwen Cohen

Dr Bronwen Cohen is Chief Executive of 'Children in Scotland', the national agency representing over 350 organisations and professionals working with children and their families throughout Scotland. She is a member of the Scottish Executive's Expert Reference Group for the Cabinet Sub-Group on Children's Services and a Visiting Professor at the Thomas Coram Research Institute of Education at the University of London.

Sue Dumbleton

Sue Dumbleton works for the Open University in Scotland as a Staff Tutor in the Faculty of Health and Social Care. She has previously taught in schools, further and adult education and has worked in a wide range of social care and social work settings. She has a long association with PLUS as a parent of a service-user and a member of the Board of Directors.

Ann Glaister

Ann Glaister (formerly Brechin) was a clinical psychologist working with children and families before joining The Open University's Faculty of Health and Social Care in 1978. She has written on disability and care issues and served as Sub Dean for a number of years before retiring at the end of 2004.

Bob Glaister

Bob Glaister taught English in the Borders before joining The Open University in Scotland as Staff Tutor (Education) in 1971, subsequently a Senior Lecturer. He served as Dean of the School of Education from 1990 to 1998 and led the development of the OU's Chartered Teacher programme before retiring at the end of 2004.

Douglas Hutchison

Douglas Hutchison worked as an RE teacher, then in a residential school for young people experiencing social, emotional and behavioural difficulties. He subsequently worked as a behaviour support teacher, before training as an educational psychologist. He currently works in the South Ayrshire psychological service.

Jeannie Mackenzie

After thirteen years of teaching in primary and special schools, Jeannie Mackenzie became involved in home–school community partnerships, and was principal officer of the Home School Employment Partnership in Ferguslie Park, then an integration manager during the pilot phase of Integrated Community Schools and is now a Quality Improvement Officer in the Education Department of East Renfrewshire Council.

Chris Wiles

Dr Chris Wiles is a clinical psychologist working at the Rowan Centre, a busy and dynamic child and adolescent mental health service in Moray in the north east of Scotland. He studied and worked in Aberdeen and Glasgow before returning home, hailing from Elgin originally. He is a committed service developer and, clinically, his interests are in systemic practice, family approaches and autism spectrum disorders.

INTRODUCTION

Ann Glaister and Bob Glaister

For more than a decade now there has been, across the UK, an increasing trend for government to encourage providers of services, in the widest sense, to work more collaboratively, to pool resources, to form partnerships. It could be argued that in the first place this was driven by a cost-cutting agenda or indeed by a political desire to reduce the power and influence of, say, local authorities or professional bodies. However the new Scottish Parliament, itself run by a coalition government, has embraced this approach wholeheartedly as the way to develop its key aspirations to raise the quality of service provision and facilitate social inclusion. The Parliament is therefore enacting positively one of its founding principles that it should be 'accessible, open, responsive and develop procedures which make possible a participative approach to the development, consideration and scrutiny of policy and legislation' (Scottish Office, 1998c, p. 3) so that Bloomer, albeit from a local authority perspective, can say:

> collaboration in the design and delivery of public services is a central government priority. Partnership working is a way of taking it forward in circumstances where central government is unwilling to extend the remit of local authorities. (Bloomer, 2003, p. 164)

There is a growing literature on partnership in general: its forms, definitions, costs, benefits, contexts, etc. And there is beginning to appear some evaluation of the policies in Scotland. But while policy is national, implementation is local, having to take account of local constraints and opportunities, and being implemented by individual practitioners. There is a great deal of activity under way, but not yet much sharing of experience or opportunity to reflect upon that activity. The intention of this volume is to convey a sense of the experience of what is happening on the ground and to illustrate the impact at operational/practitioner level. The book will not provide an exhaustive overview, but rather it is an opportunity for a selected range of contributors to describe what seem to be the important aspects of some of the very different developments involved in one of the most important policy areas for the new Parliament — children's services.

This volume, therefore, attempts to

- outline how policy is developing in the context of children's services in Scotland;
- illustrate some of the activity in various fields;
- draw out some of the implications of inter-agency collaboration in practice — what issues arise and what lessons can be learned.

The first chapter is designed to provide an overview of policy developments in relation to children's services in Scotland. This is quite a gargantuan task, but we have been fortunate that Bronwen Cohen, Chief Executive of Children in Scotland, agreed to contribute. The intention is to provide a summary that will be meaningful to practitioners, particularly those in first line management or professional leadership roles, who may find themselves drawn into new kinds of practice roles and relationships without a full understanding of the whole picture. There then follow four case studies and a final chapter in which we pull out some of the themes and issues about inter-agency collaboration which arise from the case studies. We also consider some of the theoretical underpinnings concerned with how we provide for children and young people which will better relate to the questions: what is being learned about inter-agency collaboration in Scotland and what might facilitate progress?

The case studies focus upon different aspects of services for children: for all children and young people, including disabled children and children with mental health problems, in mainstream school education and in the early years, within and outwith formal school settings. They cover different parts of the country, from Moray to Ayrshire; different perspectives, for example, local authorities and voluntary organisations; and different backgrounds, for example, parents/users and professionals, in particular from health, education and social work. The authors were invited, in broad terms, to consider the nature of the collaboration/integration, to reflect upon their experience to date, and to review what has been learned about collaborative/integrative services. We hope that this illustrates how policies are being mediated through the activities and experiences of individuals and their relationships on a day-to-day basis, and therefore the impact on the individual practitioner.

It is perhaps not insignificant that one of the core competences to be displayed by the newly created Chartered Teacher is 'working with others'. This will be essential if the high profile development of New, now entitled Integrated, Community Schools is to succeed. (We use ICS for both.) The ICS initiative has already received some close scrutiny at local level, for example the report by Baron *et al.* (2003) on Glasgow's Learning Communities, Allan *et al.* (2004) and McCulloch *et al.* (2004). We shall take account of relevant findings from these ICS evaluations in our final chapter, but we chose our case studies with a wider frame of reference in mind than children in schools. Certainly Jeannie Mackenzie is an Integration Manager for ICS, and she takes an authority perspective with illustrations from both primary and secondary schools in East Renfrewshire, but she engages excitingly with the contributions from other than teachers. South Ayrshire has now 'clustered' its schools in line with ICS developments, but, as well, it has arranged within the clusters its approach for pre-school children with additional needs. Douglas Hutchison, an educational psychologist, outlines the role of an Early Years Forum. The third study is a targeted or specialist service, but non-statutory, and in it Sue Dumbleton, writing as both a parent and a social worker, describes the impact of a voluntary group which pioneered formal support for play opportunities for disabled young people in Stirlingshire and forged partnerships with the local authority. Fourthly, as *For Scotland's Children* (Scottish Executive, 2001c) acknowledged the importance of both Education and Health in children's services, we offer a study which originates principally in Health but is attempting to co-operate sensitively with other services: Chris Wiles, a clinical psychologist, writes about mental health services for young people in Moray and the move towards greater collaboration with schools.

We hope that these case studies will all throw light on the issues of inter-agency collaboration which will arise in the implementation of the Scottish Executive's vision of integration:

> despite their different history, boundaries and legislative require-ments, children's services — encompassing education, child welfare, social work, health, leisure and recreation services for children from birth to 18 years — should consider themselves as a single unitary system. (Scottish Executive, 2001c)

CHAPTER 1

INTER-AGENCY COLLABORATION IN CONTEXT: THE 'JOINING-UP' AGENDA

Bronwen Cohen

Meanings and definitions

'Inter-agency collaboration' is one of many terms denoting new and closer relationships between and within services. 'Inter-agency collaboration', 'multi-agency', 'joined-up', 'child-centred services', 'integrated' or 'partnership' working: these are terms which now trip off our tongues and jump out of policy and guidance documents.

These phrases relate to process — the means used to achieve an end. The end itself may not always be clear and can vary considerably. The envisaged goal may be to ensure that those working in one area have an understanding, and take account, of what is happening in other services or other aspects of children's lives and at different stages of their lives. It may be that there are objectives — for example, promoting healthy eating amongst children — which require a shared approach across those working with children at different ages or during different parts of their day, at school, within social activities or other services or at home with their families. It can mean ensuring that all services are alert to identifying those children requiring special protection or support. It may mean dividing responsibilities for providing support — and ensuring that there is no duplication or inconsistency of approach. It can involve — as we see later — the development of a common 'vision' for all those providing services to children.

It can in some instances go further than all of these and mean 'integrating' or 'merging' separately delivered services. This may be because delivering some services separately does not make much sense. For example, as the Scottish Childcare Strategy asserted, 'day care and early education are interdependent' (Scottish Office, 1998a, para. 1.6).

It may be that the goal of a 'whole child' approach (recognising a child's physical, emotional, social and educational needs) requires not just collaboration but ensuring that children's needs are met in one service and not several. Or it may be the difficulties of providing services separately — the economics of services can look very different in rural areas.

Sometimes the terms are used in a way which suggests they are an end in themselves or as though the processes described in terms such as 'collaboration', 'partnership' and 'integration' are synonymous.

'Joining-up' is used here in a generic sense to denote the development of a wide range of relationships intended to promote closer and more effective working between services. 'Inter-agency collaboration' is used to refer to a relationship between agencies and services which may involve collaboration in planning, working together on specific issues or projects, or the sharing of posts. 'Integration' is used to refer to the 'merger' or 'fusion' of services across a number of conceptual and structural dimensions. (See Cohen *et al.*, 2004, pp. 8–9 for a fuller analysis.)

A little history

When did it all start? Looked at from the perspective of the twenty-first century, some early services such as Robert Owen's pioneering Institution for the Formation of Character were examples of 'integration' (and 'life-long learning') in action. Owen's Institution and associated infant school, which opened in 1816, provided for children from 18 months to 12 years of age and their parents and other employees outside working hours, combining the functions of care and education of children — alongside 'community' education with classes for their parents and young people (Cohen, 2002, pp. 18–21).

As the state became involved in education, services developed within separate administrative and legislative frameworks. The 1872 Education (Scotland) Act set the age of compulsory schooling at 5–13 years; the 1918 Education (Scotland) Act empowered local authorities to establish nursery schools for children over 2 and under 5 years old for those 'whose attendance at such a school is necessary or desirable for their healthy physical and mental development' (1918 Education (Scotland) Act ch. 48, part 8). State involvement and legislative provision for some aspects of education as well as health and welfare services developed more slowly. Adult (later community) education was first referred to in legislation in 1934 under the Adult Education (Scotland) Regulations 1934/1343 (S.72), which empowered education authorities to co-operate with voluntary bodies in securing adult education provision and was a concept further developed by the 1945 Education (Scotland) Act. The health of school children was considered in 1906 and 1907: legislation in these years related to free school meals and a school medical service but a national health service was only established following the Second World War.

Over time — and the last half century in particular — the number and range of services for children, young people and their families has increased considerably. Over the same period the relationship between these services has attracted more and more attention. An early seminal report in this respect was the 1964 report by Lord Kilbrandon who chaired a committee on juvenile justice. His report was notable not only for its recommendation of a new justice system for children (later to become known as children's panels) but also for his recognition of the role played by different services in juvenile justice and the importance of ensuring effective relationships between them.

> . . . it seems to us that the juvenile panels must have available to them the services, first, of all the statutory and voluntary agencies whose work is such as to bring them into frequent contact with the family, and who may be looked upon as primary sources of identification. The police are obviously one such source; among others, perhaps the most obvious are the schools, general medical practitioners, health visitors and district nursing services . . . In what is in each case probably a numerically less extensive field, ministers and priests, children's officers, probation officers, local authority health and welfare officers, and school welfare and attendance officers, in the course of their duties are also likely to identify children in need or difficulty. (Kilbrandon Report, 1964, part three, chapter XII, para. 235)

The Kilbrandon Report identified the need for what was described as a 'matching field organisation' of services (including preventive services) to support the operation of the 'juvenile panels'. It recommended that these should be established as 'social education' departments within local education authorities. The report envisaged that social education departments would be headed up by a depute director under the Director of Education and would be 'recognised as the focal point for information about all cases of children in need' (Kilbrandon Report, 1964, part three, chapter XII, para. 235). It rejected the argument that placing responsibility in the hands of education authorities — rather than local authority children's committees — might result in an overburdening of those and result in the significance of the relationships between education and the area receiving inadequate attention:

> It may be that in the past the emphasis within the Scottish educational curriculum, with its fairly strong academic bias, lent encouragement to the view that education could be treated as a formal process of learning, in that sense divorced from the wider aim of training and social living. In so far as such attitudes exist, they are, we consider, rapidly disappearing. (Kilbrandon Report, 1964, part three, chapter XII, para. 245)

In the event, a change of government brought a different approach to the 'matching field organisation of services' and the 1968 Social Work (Scotland) Act provided for separate, wide ranging social work departments for people of all ages. The new departments were given responsibility for the new children's hearing system as well as responsibility for providing and co-ordinating social work services. In addition, Section 12 (1) of the Act placed a general duty on local authorities to 'promote social welfare'. The new duty 'unequalled in other parts of UK legislation' in enabling what was described in relevant Scottish Office guidance as supporting initiatives to strengthen community resources and networks (Tisdall, 1997, p. 12) stimulated the development of services. However the establishment of the new departments also soon created new administrative barriers.

> Co-ordination with, and call on, education resources soon became an issue. Co-ordination was also problematic with health, which did not have the same administrative boundaries as local authorities. (Tisdall, 1997, p. 31)

Whilst the role of schools in relation to the juvenile justice system had formed the basis for Kilbrandon's recommendation for social education departments, other areas and aspects of divided responsibilities were attracting attention. Provision for young children was one such area. Increasing numbers of lone parents and rising rates of maternal employment focused attention on the paucity and fragmented structure of pre-school services and raised questions about the role of schools outside school hours. In 1986, Scotland's largest local authority, the former Strathclyde Regional Council, launched its Pre-Fives Initiative giving its Education Department responsibility for all pre-fives education and care services, seeking to make nursery schools the basis of flexible integrated provision such as community nurseries (Cohen *et al.*, 2004, p. 96). The Pre-Fives Unit's first Director has recalled the account she was given at the time of how it came about:

> The Leader of Strathclyde Regional Council was visiting a local nursery school, which shared a common fence with a social work day nursery. The fence was newly painted and (the councillor) got white paint on his jacket. There was then an argument between the head of the nursery school and the officer in charge of the day nursery about whether it was nursery school white paint or day nursery white paint. At this point (the councillor) exploded and the Strathclyde pre-fives strategy was born. (Penn, 2002, p. 14)

Another area which drew attention to relationships between services was that of provision for children with disabilities or 'special needs'. The strengthening of the educational rights of these children and an increasing focus on access to mainstream services highlighted both the need for more effective collaboration between relevant agencies and ways of meeting their wider needs. Growing awareness of the poor educational outcomes of children in care attracted similar attention with a 1992 report calling for education and social work departments to review their arrangements for overseeing the educational needs of children (SWSI, 1992).

In the 1990s, the call for 'improved inter-agency working' informed the enactment in 1995 of new child welfare legislation — the 1995 Children (Scotland) Act. The statutory requirement introduced by the 1968 Social Work (Scotland) Act to have separate social work and education directors had been revoked in the 1994 Local Government etc. (Scotland) Act, encouraging some rethinking of existing boundaries. The 1995 Children (Scotland) Act also followed a review of childcare law completed in 1990 which had highlighted problems arising from poor inter-agency working. As a result, the new Act sought not only to bring together separate areas of child welfare legislation but also stepped gingerly into the arena of inter-agency working, placing a statutory duty on local authorities to 'prepare, consult on and publish plans for all relevant children's services', and in guidance to the Act, pointing to the advantages of Chief Executives 'assuming corporate responsibility for plan preparation' (Children in Scotland, 1997).

The legislation had come at a time when the impact of the United Nations Convention on the Rights of the Child, ratified by the UK government in 1991, was beginning to be felt and the Convention's influence can be seen in a number of areas, most notably the recognition accorded to the welfare of the child as a paramount consideration and due regard being given to children's views in certain areas of decision making. Children are given some rights — for example, to attend their own children's hearing — but the focus of inter-agency collaboration is based on the needs rather than the rights of children. The new Act introduced into Scotland the narrower focus on 'children in need' brought in south of the border in the 1989 Children Act. This replaced the wider duty to promote social welfare which Section 12 (1) of the Social Work (Scotland) Act had given to Scottish local authorities, and almost immediately raised questions over the understanding and definitions of 'need' within different sectors. Arguably, its focus on the individual child 'in need' constrained the scope for inter-agency collaboration opened up in the same Act by the new planning duty and undermined the developing emphasis on children's rights also visible within the Act.

However, the enactment of major children's legislation in the parliamentary term prior to the 1997 election raised the profile of children's issues at a critical time. The legislative process had been notable in the degree of cross-party co-operation it engendered, and, enacted five years after equivalent legislation in England, served as a reminder of the difficulty of securing legislative time for Scottish legislation in the Westminster parliament. A number of Members of Parliament who later became Members of the Scottish Parliament — and in some cases took ministerial office — were involved in the passage of the Bill, and heard the concerns over inter-agency working. This, combined with what was to become a UK-wide 'modernising government' agenda with its emphasis on developing client-focused public services, helped to establish it as a priority for the incoming administration.

The 'joining-up' agenda post-1997

One such Member of Parliament was Sam Galbraith. Said to have coined the phrase 'joined-up working' whilst still a member of the Westminster Parliament, he subsequently became Scotland's first Minister for Children and Education (a title later changed by his successor and now Minister for Education and Young People). The change of name accompanied a major reorganisation of departmental responsibilities begun following the 1997 election and completed after the establishment of the Scottish Executive in 1999 when a new Scottish Executive department integrated responsibilities for education, childcare and child and family welfare within one department. The department, known as the Scottish Executive Education Department (SEED) brought in a new Children and Young People's Group alongside the existing Schools Group and took out higher education to become the responsibility of another minister. Writing shortly after the Children and Young People's Group had been set up, its then head described it as 'offering new opportunities for better integration of both policy and funding'.

> It should mean a more fully integrated approach to the needs of children and young people in the critical early years of life, in the pre-school years and at the important transition points as they move towards adulthood and independence . . . the new group will sit alongside and work closely with the Schools Group . . . This reflects a crucially important principle: that what happens to young people in school and outside school is related and independent. (Stewart, G., cited in Cohen, 2003, p. 239)

The reorganisation followed the launch — prior to the establishment of the Scottish Parliament — of the New Community Schools Pilot Programme (now being rolled out to all schools). This programme, although piloted in areas 'where the challenge is greatest', was envisaged as offering 'a new approach to identifying and meeting the needs of every child by organising and focusing the services which support children and their families *from their earliest years* through their development and education' (Cohen *et al.*, 2004, p. 104, emphasis added). They were, said the then Secretary of State, Donald Dewar, likely to have lessons 'of practical importance to all schools and to all having contact with young people' (Cohen *et al.*, 2004, p. 104).

The programme drew on the vision of schools as institutions for delivering lifelong and community learning, which as Wilkinson has pointed out was central to the Third Way political system expounded by Anthony Giddens, a major influence on the new government (Wilkinson, 2003, p. 22). A Scottish Executive initiated National Debate on Education in 2002 later encouraged a further rethinking of the role of schools. The then Minister for Education and Young People described the debate as intended to engage people in thinking not only about how learning and teaching are delivered but also

> about how to develop a 'whole child' approach on education, on how other professionals might work in schools and what children should be learning not just in an academic context but also in a broader social context. (Cohen *et al.*, 2004, pp. 108–9)

And the Scottish Executive response noted the need for

> radical new thinking about the way we design, build and manage our schools, about the way teachers teach, about the curriculum, and about the interaction between pupils, parents, community and school. (Cohen *et al.*, 2004, p. 109)

But the ability of schools to rethink their role in the way implied by these statements would prove to be constrained by an absence of corresponding radicalism in Early Years' policies — and on-going confusion over where responsibilities for these services lies: Holyrood or Westminster.

Departmental reorganisation in the new Scottish Executive followed the publication of the 1998 Scottish Childcare Strategy which had referred to the need for 'better integration of early education and child-care' (Scottish Office, 1998a), and the restructuring in 1999 brought together for the first time pre-school and school-age childcare and early education alongside schools within the same department. Integration of these services was high on the agenda. A year earlier, the then Minister, Sam Galbraith, told a local authorities and Early Years' conference: 'Read my lips, integration, integration, integration' (Cohen, 1998). Departmental reorganisation the following year should have assisted this process. Five years on the division still bears the name Early Education and Childcare, signalling a continuing conceptual divide between educa-tion and care for young children. Part of the reason for this lies in the limited public funding for the 'universal' dimension within Early Years' services. This has been largely restricted to supporting a part-time pre-school place for 3- and 4-year-olds, reasonable as a first step but to date not extended despite criticism by the Organisation for Economic Co-operation and Development (OECD, 2001). Other funding has been largely restricted to supporting disadvantaged groups and areas and promoting employment amongst these groups. The development of serv-ices for children and parents outside these areas has been left to the market, stimulated through tax credits and other measures. The nature of these policies has meant that in reality the lead in 'childcare' policies has come from the Westminster Parliament, not only in those areas reserved to it but also in others including, for example, the Sure Start initiative.

Ambiguities and fault lines in Early Years' policy have inhibited the development of what the OECD has described as the development of 'strong and equal relationship' between new — now called integrated — community schools and early childhood services. New relationships have been forged with some services but their contribution to the lifelong learning agenda, whilst visible within local initiatives such as Glasgow's new learning communities has to date been less clearly articulated. Scotland's inclusion in an Extended Schools Childcare Pilot Scheme announced in 2004 by the Department of Work and Pensions is likely to stimulate the involvement of schools in pre-school and school-age childcare but as an 'add on' service, separately funded and separately provided. It sits oddly with the more 'organic' approach to relationships between schools and other services raised by the National Education Debate and implied by the Scottish Executive's response to this.

Whilst the 'integrative' agenda within Early Years' education and care slowed, 'joining up' was already moving on and widening out. In 2001, the Scottish Executive set up a review to look at ways of better integrating children's services. The review team, drawn from local government, the National Health Service (NHS) and the voluntary sector concluded that services had often been badly co-ordinated and 'chaotic' with some children 'born to fail' and some invisible to services. It proposed an action plan for achieving better integration at a local level. Most significantly, the report argued that

> despite their different history, boundaries and legislative requirements, children's services — encompassing education, child welfare, social work, health, leisure and recreation services for children from birth to 18 years — should consider themselves as a single unitary system.

It also recommended that health should take the co-ordinating role for services for children under 5, and education for children from 5 to 18 years (Scottish Executive, 2001c). In response to the report, Scottish Executive ministers announced the establishment of a ministerial task force to 'drive forward progress on integrated children's services', and subsequently established a Children and Young People Cabinet Delivery group to further develop this 'integrative' agenda. The group is chaired by the Minister for Education and Young People, and includes the First Minister, Deputy First Minister and relevant portfolio ministers for Health, Justice, Communities, Culture and Sport and Finance. It has the following priority work streams for 'cross-portfolio activity':

- ensuring a shared vision of aspirations and expectations for children and young people, across universal and targeted services;
- working to improve delivery by reducing bureaucracy and ensuring effective arrangements for funding, planning and joint working;
- developing a coherent system for assessment and information sharing to ensure children and young people receive the support they need;

- establishing joint inspection and quality assurance systems to support and encourage continuous improvement across children's services;
- developing our understanding of the children's workforce requirements to ensure that it has the skills, qualifications, capacity and leadership it needs.

> (Scottish Executive, 27 May 2004, letter to chief executives of Scottish Local Authorities and Chief Executives of NHS Boards)

The wider 'joining-up' agenda will shortly see the publication of an Integrated Strategy for the Early Years, expected to cover the age range 0–6 years (rather than 0–5 as initially stated), and proposing a set of common agreed outcomes across all services covering children's health, social and emotional development and ability to learn. 'Social and emotional development' is defined as including improving children's self-esteem, confidence and independence (Scottish Executive presentation at Children in Scotland seminar 'School as the hub', Stranraer, September 2004).

The joining-up agenda has also seen the establishment of community health partnerships intended not only to have responsibility for a wide range of community health provision such as general practitioner (GP) services and community nursing but also to secure improvements in health through partnerships, with amongst others, schools. For example, every school in Scotland has been set the target of becoming a health promoting school by 2007 and nutritional guidance developed for school lunches. Revised guidance in 2004 for all local agencies on planning and delivering children's services seeks to

> rationalise existing national planning and monitoring requirements on local authorities, health boards and their local partners for education improvement, child health, children's services and youth justice into a single integrated planning process. (Scottish Executive, 27 May 2004)

A strategic vision statement offers a vision of shared expectations and aspirations for children and young people across all agencies and sectors and the future programme envisaged includes further work on accountability and integration, co-terminosity, supporting parents and carers and workforce reform (Scottish Executive, 2004a).

The 'joining-up' agenda: the impact

There can be little doubt that the 'joining-up' agenda has focused attention on the relationship between different sectors, agencies and professions working with children, young people and their families. Calls for inter-agency collaboration have now translated into national policies and programmes. The boundaries between sectors and services have begun to be redrawn and new planning guidance — within children's services and across communities — offers a powerful framework for progressing the vision of children's services as a 'single integrated planning system'.

> New organisational structures have emerged and are still developing: integrated community schools; learning communities; childcare partnerships; community health partnerships and child protection committees — on which new draft guidance strengthens the involvement of local authority and independent education service. (Scottish Executive, 2004b, p. 16)

New jobs have developed — some, such as 'integration managers' reflecting the collaborative agenda. New relationships are being forged, both horizontally with other service-providers, and, somewhat more slowly, vertically — as in the learning communities now being developed in a number of areas in Scotland.

The 'change' agenda has reflected not just a concern to improve the relationship between services but is also seeing the slow emergence of a new relationship with children themselves — now more likely to be listened to or given the right to take action on their own behalf. As we have seen, the 1995 Children (Scotland) Act had made some provision for this within child welfare. New education legislation enacted in 2000 similarly showed some recognition of children having a voice and rights stipulating that education authorities must pay 'due regard' to the views of the child or young person in decisions that significantly affect them and gives children themselves the right to appeal their exclusion from school. The Act also confers a right on every child of school age to receive school education directed towards the 'development of the personality, talents and mental and physical abilities of the child and young person to their fullest potential' (Children in Scotland, 2000, pp. 6–7). This right has been strengthened by the 2004 Additional Support for Learning Act which places duties on other relevant agencies including social work services and health to help education authorities meet their duties to support 'any child or young person who, for whatever reason, requires additional support' (Scottish Executive, 2004c). The appointment of a Children's Commissioner and a 'vision' statement issued in 2004, which makes reference to the United Nations Convention on the Rights of the Child, are likely to assist this process, offering a welcome, if tentative, emphasis on 'rights' rather than 'needs'.

Relationships, roles and responsibilities are changing. Nevertheless, there are some striking continuities in some policies which shape the context for children's services. As we have seen, these have included an emphasis on targeting, a reliance on the market to provide 'childcare' and, associated with this, a continuing 'unequal' relationship between schools and services, undermining the visions of 'life-long learning' and 'single unitary system' aspired to within Scottish Executive policies and making workforce reform a more distant prospect. Is there any prospect for changing this? I have argued elsewhere that one of the problems lies in a continuing Westminster influence on key aspects of early years policy, which has locked Scotland into market-led HM Treasury-determined childcare policies and limited the impact of its educational initiatives (Cohen *et al.*, 2004). At the time of writing, in the run up to the 2005 Westminster elections, there were signs that a major re-think was under way on early years policy south of the border. English ministers had visited Sweden. The Swedish model of universal entitlement for children from 12 months to 12 years of age to pre-school and 'freetime' (school age childcare) services and 'whole day schools' was described by the journalist who accompanied one of them as 'distant but perhaps less impossible for a third term Labour regime'. Former cabinet minister Stephen Byers, working on the Labour manifesto, wrote of the need 'to ensure an equal start by caring for children from different economic groups in the same place' and the need to move beyond 'a highly targeted approach' (Cohen, 2004, pp. 36–7). A commitment has been made to rolling out the children's centres established in disadvantaged areas in England. A shift to subsidising services rather than parents through tax credits may serve to repatriate Early Years' policy to Scotland — and make possible a more radical approach to the understanding of 'community' within integrated community schools.

The 'joining-up' agenda: the challenge for schools

As other chapters in this book demonstrate, 'joining-up' in various forms is in growing evidence. This chapter has examined some of the key developments shaping the policy context and identified some of the constraints, particularly at a national level. But perhaps the biggest challenge lies in schools themselves. Radical Swedish reforms were motivated not only by the idea of children experiencing 'an integrated school day with education and care in one setting and an integrated educational career from age one to age 16', but also by the belief that integrating pre-school and school-age childcare systems with schools would change schools (Cohen *et al.*, 2004, p. 154). The 'whole child' approach in which the former Minister of Education and Young People hoped to engage people requires recognition that, as one Swedish trainer put it, 'Learning is just one theoretical way of constructing life. The hands, the heart and the head (must all be addressed) — but the heart cannot be forgotten' (Cohen *et al.*, 2004, p. 173).

The closer the relationship between services the greater the challenge. But the benefits can be enormous. Drumchapel New Learning Community in Glasgow is discovering that vertical links have much to offer in addressing issues such as attendance, health and parenting across pre-school, primary and secondary schools. As the head of the Drumchapel Family Centre has commented, attendance problems and issues around parental involvement do not just start with school:

if we can establish a good routine of attendance when children are very young, this has a positive impact on their attendance rates when they start school. Likewise if we are able to engage their parents very early on, they are more likely to play an active role in their child's education when they start school. (Children in Scotland, 2004, p. 13)

Such relationships between services go beyond Lord Kilbrandon's recommendations 'for a matching field organisation' of services and suggest the possibility that if mind sets can change we may yet realise the vision of a recent Minister for Education and Young People of achieving a 'whole child' approach to children's services.

CHAPTER 2

A MODEL FOR EDUCATIONAL CHANGE IN EAST RENFREWSHIRE

Jeannie Mackenzie

Once upon a time there was a small village on the edge of a river. One day a villager noticed a baby floating down the river. He jumped into the river and saved the baby from drowning.

The next day this same villager noticed two babies in the river. He called for help, and both babies were rescued from the swift waters. The following day four babies were rescued. Then eight babies, then more, and still more.

The villagers organised themselves, setting up watchtowers and training teams of swimmers to rescue babies. Groups were trained to give mouth-to-mouth resuscitation. Others provided food and clothing for the chilled babies. Still others provided foster homes.

Although the babies could not all be saved, the villagers felt they were doing well to save as many as they could each day. One day, however, someone asked, 'Where are all these babies coming from? Who is throwing them into the river? Why? Let's go upstream and sort it out up there.' But other villagers asked, 'If we go upstream who will rescue these babies? We all have specialised jobs to do here.'

And so the numbers of babies in the river increased daily. Those saved increased, but those who drowned increased even more.

Traditional African tale

Introduction

The concept of 'up-streaming' has been around for some time in the field of health, education and of community development. Although few people would disagree that work with children benefits from early inter-vention, up-streaming gives rise to expressions of concern that scarce resources may be diverted from mainstream services. However, such expressions may mask deeper objections to up-streaming because of the challenge it poses to organisational culture and professional identity.

The Scottish Office policy of integrated community schools (ICS) (Scottish Office, 1998a) was bold in its allocation of 'upstream' funding to improve educational, health and social outcomes. The prospectus set out an ambitious three-year programme to raise educational standards and promote social inclusion. Designed to tackle the root causes of low attainment at source, the programme majored on the child in the family and the community, focusing not only on educational programmes, but on social support, health and community participation. In doing so, the prospectus inherently challenged the organisational and professional culture of school education, health and social services, and clearly identified the twin aims of raising educational standards and promoting social inclusion as two sides of the same coin.

Although the Scottish Office Prospectus set out the essential characteristics of ICS, considerable scope was permitted for developing local solutions to local issues. Thus the ICS projects developed in very different ways in local situations, posing real difficulties in determining national trends, but offering a rich fund of varying experience from which lessons may be learned.

The case study presented in this chapter seeks to consider the distinctive route taken in one local authority; the challenges experienced along the road, the lessons learned and plans for the future. There is no suggestion that the route taken has been the only one or even the most effective one. However, a case will be made that there has been a real change in organisational and professional culture and professional identity. There has been a change in how the role of the school in the community is conceived and how the learner is regarded. To create the right conditions for such a change to happen, the initiative was guided by Fullan's model of educational change (Fullan, 1993), and local practice will be discussed within this model.

Fullan associated eight lessons with successful educational change, that is:

1. The more complex a change the less you can force it.
2. Change is a journey, not a blueprint.
3. Problems are our friends.
4. Premature vision blinds.
5. Individualism and collectivism must have equal power.
6. Both top down and bottom up strategies are necessary.
7. Connection with the wider environment is critical for success.
8. Every person is a change agent — change is too important to leave to the experts.

Three areas are discussed in relation to the change process in East Renfrewshire; these are the changes that schools have made in moving:

- from home linking to family learning;
- from referrals to remote services to school-based support; and
- towards becoming health promoting schools.

Bordering the southwest side of the city of Glasgow, East Renfrewshire covers an area of around 18,000 hectares and has a population of almost 89,000. It encompasses a diverse range of environments, including urban, suburban and rural areas. Overall, East Renfrewshire is perceived as a prosperous area, with high levels of home and car ownership. However, this perception masks the detail of real inequalities in income, housing and health. In spite of these inequalities, the attainment levels of the children in East Renfrewshire schools are among the best in Scotland, and many schools serving areas of multiple disadvantages consistently outperform their national equivalents. The introduction of community schooling in 1999 offered the Council a prospect of closing the opportunity gap still further. There were two pilot initiatives, one in the urban area of Thornliebank and one in the village of Neilston. The lessons that have been learnt from the approach are now being applied across all 32 schools and 5 nurseries.

From home linking to family learning

> The common way to think about literacy is to see it as a ladder. This ladder begins at school . . . the emphasis is, therefore, on standardising literacy accomplishments through the use of tests, defining core skills, and pre-specifying learning outcomes . . . these frameworks do not recognise the validity of peoples' own definitions, uses and aspirations for literacy, with the result that they disempower . . . they define what counts as real literacy and silence everything else. (Tett, 2002, p. 28)

The process of developing the concept of family learning in East Renfrewshire has developed gradually since 1999, when the first ICS initiative was established. Early conceptions of the role of ICS with parents were based on a deficit model, with the school being understood as the source of knowledge and learning. The school curriculum was regarded as central to the role, and the post was therefore envisaged as requiring professional skills that only a teacher could supply. An examination of the first job description for an ICS 'Home School Link Teacher' reveals that the discourse prevalent at the time was based on the 'ladder' approach to learning; the teacher was expected to 'give parents advice on behaviour management' and 'provide guidance to parents on the 5–14 curriculum'.

Rather than proceeding blindly with a 'premature vision', the Steering Group for the pilot initiative approved a redrafting of the job description, permitting a wider understanding of family and community engagement. The ICS prospectus helped redefine early thinking; the essential characteristic of family and community 'engagement' suggested a wider professional role, where skills in engaging with others, empowering individuals, group and team working were required. The post was redefined for a family learning co-ordinator with a broader remit and a broader range of qualifications from which a candidate could be appointed, including teaching, social work and community education.

The model of family learning that has developed recognises the strength of learning at home and in the community. It challenges traditional practice in parental involvement, where parents are corralled into manageable groups to sanction school policy, raise funds, attend curriculum workshops, mix paint, put on aprons, and make sure the children have done their homework. By failing to value community skills, these practices tend to disempower, disengage and disaffect. Instead family learning affirms parents as educators, and values family involvement in learning over parental involvement in schools.

In East Renfrewshire under ICS, the chief vehicle for family engagement has been the permanent appointment of the family learning co-ordinators, who have used professional skills gained in community education, community arts, teaching and literacy to develop imaginative approaches and build partnerships. The diversity of approaches at first caused confusion. 'Shouldn't they all work in the same way?' was a frequent plea and 'Surely we should be taking a team approach?' However, Fullan argues that in pursuing only collective approaches we risk losing the imaginative power of individual thinking and responses. This is best explained through two very different examples of family learning in context. Both came into being as the result of creative individual enterprise, but both are now sustained through developing team approaches, with teaching staff taking an increasingly significant role. Both examples comprise significant involvement with children; one of the most successful means of engaging parents has been through provision for their children.

Circus skills developed in Thornliebank Primary as a response to pupil consultation, in which the activity was voted the most desirable from a wide range of choices of after school activities. In this instance, children were themselves agents of change; the opportunity they had to choose circus skills for themselves resulted in a programme that has lasted five years, involved around 300 children, and has been a catalyst for engaging many of their parents in a much wider range of family learning activities.

The circus skills workshops, provided by family learning co-ordinators, health promotion co-ordinators and teachers, are designed to be a fun way of encouraging the children to consider and support one another, to take part in healthy exercise and build a broad range of skills. Developing listening skills, self-confidence and teamwork are all part of the circus approach. Balance and co-ordination are practised, with children devising their own routines and with the emphasis on participation as well as demonstration of skills. Children learn that good teamwork and mutual support are vital for performance — when there are difficulties within the group these are resolved through use of a circle time. There is therefore a strong educational focus within the activity.

The second example is of the Families Reading Together programme. The teaching of reading was a key priority in the development plan of Thornliebank Primary. The ICS contribution aimed to release the potential of family literacy. The approach recognises that although we all accept that the reading children do out of school is invaluable in helping them develop good literacy skills for later life, not all children have a positive experience of reading in their early years. Sometimes the barrier to reading together is lack of awareness of its importance, but more often it is occasioned by issues associated with poverty: lack of access to books in the home, lack of parental literacy, lack of confidence in reading skills or the stress of living in poverty.

The family learning co-ordinator is central to the Families Reading Together programme; indeed the nursery children christened him as 'Mr Pick-a Book'! Story telling is used in the nursery to open up the world of pleasure in books and children from nursery to Primary 3 have a weekly opportunity to choose a high quality book to take home. The book is accompanied by a notebook for parents, which encourages parents to read to their child and invites comments on how both enjoyed the story. Rigorous records are kept of the issue of books and of parental engagement in the process, and this engagement has consistently been high.

From Primary 4 to Primary 7, paired reading techniques are used to engage parents to read with their children. Again, good quality books are available in a range of reading levels and a wide range of interest, with parents and children being invited to comment on their experience. Through inter-agency collaboration, the library services have proved an invaluable source of good quality books, and story-telling workshops, for children and for parents. The core programme is supplemented by special reading sessions for youngsters who give cause for concern in the tracking of reading; these are relaxed, fun sessions, often over the lunch period. The bi-lingual family learning co-ordinator provides informal sessions for parents who require support with English as a second language.

In an evaluation of the programme in its first year, parents reported that their children showed increasing interest in reading. They also reported that they spend more time reading stories with their child and that the family was more likely to visit the public library, and to read themselves, all as a result of the programme. Now in its fourth year, the programme has demonstrated that parents who are successfully engaged in reading for pleasure with their children at the nursery stage remain engaged as their child moves through into the third year in primary.

In a large scale study of parental engagement in British Columbia, Coleman discredits a series of myths that he suggests teachers hold about parental involvement (Coleman, 1998). One of these is the myth of the parent who is uninterested in their child's learning. The experience of programmes such as circus skills and families reading together also question the myth — could the truth be that there are no uninterested parents; only methods of working with parents that inhibit positive responses by defining and limiting learning in terms of school curriculum? Changing school approaches to parental engagement cannot be forced, however. The successful demonstration of effective approaches, sometimes over a number of years, can be more powerful in changing professional cultures.

Ultimately, however, effective approaches need to be formalised and creative approaches need to be secured through strategic planning. In East Renfrewshire, the practice of family learning is now recognised as central to the Education Department's operation, is a key element of community learning and development, is enshrined in the Corporate Strategy, and has a growing and committed team of workers whose task is not only to promote family learning, but also to encourage mainstream services, including schools, to support it too. The importance of family learning has been recognised by combining it with Sure Start funded resources into a new family learning team, with a dedicated family learning manager.

From remote services to school-based support

The notion of collaborative practice to support vulnerable children and young people is not a new one; the most effective interventions have long been recognised as the result of professional collaboration and pupil/school/parent partnership in decision making. Almost thirty years ago, the Pack report (SED, 1977) recommended multi-disciplinary teams in schools. This advice was elaborated on in the *Young People in Trouble* report (Strathclyde Region, 1987). More recently, *Better Behaviour, Better Learning* (Scottish Executive, 2001a) and *Alternatives to School Exclusion* (HMIE, 2000) strongly advocated collaborative practice. Connection with the wider environment is understood in these documents as critical to changing schools' capacity to meet the needs of the most vulnerable. Within ICS, however, these connections are understood to be about more than inter-agency collaboration and planning, they also involve joint delivery of supportive programmes, participation, appreciation of the home and community setting and participation in by children, young people and their families.

In East Renfrewshire, multi-agency groups that had been put in place at the time of the *Young People in Trouble* report provided a base and springboard for extending support. In 1999, these groups existed in some secondary schools and consisted mainly of teaching staff, educational psychologists and a link social worker visiting from the area team. The ability of the group to respond to the range of issues presented expanded sharply with the advent of the ICS school-based social workers. In an example of how 'top down' strategies are critical for success, the Social Work Department's courageous response to ICS was to make permanent, school-based appointments of social workers. These staff were dedicated to early intervention and did not routinely become involved in statutory casework.

This bold approach caused problems in the early days; questions were raised in the Department as to how such social workers were to be adequately supervised and whether the isolation from their social work colleagues would inevitably lead to them becoming de-skilled and de-professionalised. Within schools, there were concerns about explaining to parent groups the presence of a social worker on the staff team and issues of confidentiality. Sometimes the friction between different professional codes led to philosophical discussions on the central role of the school and social work, more often it led to banal arguments over social workers taking annual leave during term time. As Fullan argues, however, problems can be our friends — it is impossible to learn without them. The discussions, negotiations (and occasionally heated arguments!) helped both social work and teaching staff reach not only a workable consensus, but also refined understandings of their joint practice and shared commitment to the child or young person.

One social worker found the experience of school-based work enhanced her understanding of teaching staff's concern for poor attendance:

> I had not appreciated before how devastating a 80% attendance rate is for a child's education — previously I had thought we should only be intervening if attendance was very low indeed. Now I recognise that losing a day a week of school is usually symptomatic of something we ought to respond to.

One depute head grew to appreciate the year round nature of the social work task:

> I still get frustrated when the social worker takes holiday during the term, but I now remember that when we all leave at the end of June, the children's need may be greater and family stress increases — someone needs to be there to bridge that gap.

School-based social workers not only introduced a new level of service, they also added another dimension to the packages of support available. Along with additional hours from Careers Scotland and the psychological service, they provided the schools with a range of tools which could be more speedily and effectively used than before. One psychologist commented:

> If I need to put a package of support together for a young person, say a college placement and some benefit support — I can do it much

quicker than before. You are not having to phone different agencies — they use the same office and we can do it there and then.

The key to breaking down the barriers to collaboration lay in joint practice. Having the courage to get involved and being willing to take a risky step into foreign territory brings newfound confidence. Demonstrating practice for one another, reflecting together on practice, and celebrating improving practice were all powerful in building collaborative teams.

The extension of multi-agency support into primary and pre-5 settings has proved popular with headteachers and with parents. Parents who would hesitate to visit a social work office seem content to access support through their child's school. Often the first professional to learn of an issue affecting the child, such as a family breakdown, chronic illness, lack of parenting skills, bereavement or homelessness is the primary head teacher; 'Meeting regularly with other professionals who can not only give advice, but actually get involved in support, means we are able to support our children much better than before.' Self-referrals from parents are a steady source of new work — parents are confident of asking for help when they know of others who have received valuable support.

Finally, collaboration is cost effective. In the first three years of the pilot schools in East Renfrewshire, there was evidence of a reduction in crisis referral to the social work department. Those involved provided two explanations: firstly, early intervention was providing support to families at an earlier stage, avoiding the need for statutory involvement — 'up-streaming' was actually freeing those downstream to deal with fewer, more serious cases. Secondly, working collaboratively was increasing the skills of all staff involved.

The more complex a change, argues Fullan, the less you can force it. Becoming a socially inclusive school is a complex process, and it cannot be forced; it must grow slowly and, at times, uncertainly. One means of advancing its growth is to encourage the expression of uncertainty; to be open about our fears and concerns, to recognise that we are on a journey that is to some extent through uncharted territory, and to affirm the pioneer spirit. Invited to share their hopes and fears for ICS in 1999, teaching staff expressed concerns that any reduction in school exclusion would lead to poor behaviour in classrooms and inferior exam results. It was vital to acknowledge and to understand these fears, and to develop the service to respond appropriately. Looking back, we can see that these fears were groundless. Woodfarm High, the only secondary school involved in the first phase of the pilot, has steadily reduced its exclusion rate from 33 exclusions in 1998/9 to 9 in 2003/4, and at the same time increased its attainment rates, staying on rates and higher and further education entrance rates. Against this backdrop of evidence, social inclusion and raising attainment (the twin objectives of ICS) are now routinely understood as two sides of the same coin. The school-based social work service will shortly be available in all seven school clusters within East Renfrewshire.

The multi-agency teams in schools are now so well received and embedded that new developments experience less resistance. The concept of a youth counselling service, conceived originally by a school-based social worker, grew quickly within this fertile environment. Teaching staff who had become comfortable working with other agencies were welcoming of another service which would help them address the complex needs of the young people. East Renfrewshire Youth Counselling Service, operated by the Renfrewshire Association for Mental Health, has four full time youth counsellors working according to British Association for Counselling and Psychotherapy guidelines and providing a service based in all seven secondaries.

Strategic planning within the education department has assisted the process of spreading good practice to schools not involved in the ICS pilot; social inclusion and integrated services became the responsibility of the quality improvement team and a dedicated member of that team now ensures connection with the wider environment of integrated children's planning, and therefore with community planning.

Health promoting schools

As a society, we place heavy expectations on our schools. We want high standards of academic achievement, but at the same time we want young people prepared for adult life and the world of work. We demand high standards of pupil behaviour, while at the same time we require excellence in pastoral care. We want pupils who conform and wear uniform, but we also want them to be creative and enterprising.

The twin objectives of ICS place an extended range of expectations on schools, to work collaboratively with other agencies and to work in partnership not only with parents, but also with the wider community. When the Scottish Executive announced in 2003 that all schools would become health promoting by 2007, it is unsurprising that this directive was not universally well received. Some regarded it as an unwelcome addition to an already overburdened set of priorities, others as a distraction from the core purpose of schooling.

Due to the support of the partner NHS boards, Greater Glasgow and Argyll and Clyde, the health promoting school model was fortunately already well established in East Renfrewshire through ICS. Three permanent health co-ordinators, part funded by the NHS, work within the education department to support schools with health promotion through staff development, consultation and joint programme delivery. The health co-ordinators had encouraged a range of health needs-based programmes and responses, aimed not only at children and young people, but also at staff, families and the wider community. These activities were firstly characterised by grass roots development, that is, they were prompted by individual organisational or community expressions of need, and were designed initially to address local problems. For example, a play leader scheme arose from teacher and parent concern about conflict in the playground, and sexual health programmes arose from teacher concern about their own staff development needs. Secondly, they were characterised by an extension of the range and degree of work that schools began to do with other agencies, as health co-ordinators successfully involved other agencies in jointly planning and delivering programmes. Thirdly, they were characterised by a strong focus on staff health and well-being, acknowledging that any organisation can only be as healthy as its staff group.

An early example of collaborative enterprise in health was the development of a school cluster approach to alcohol. The key professional was the health co-ordinator. Her skills lay in leading on joint planning from the data gathered during an earlier health needs assessment, in planning and in bringing diverse people and resources together for a common purpose. Using a curriculum pack designed by NHS Greater Glasgow Youth Health Promotion team, *Exploring Alcohol*, Woodfarm High developed with her a programme for all primary seven pupils in its associated schools. The programme is detailed below in terms of a model of the health promoting school adapted from the European Network of Health Promoting Schools (see www.euro.who.int/eprise/main/WHO/Progs/ENHPS).

Management and leadership
School management identified the need for a programme on alcohol and young people following a needs assessment exercise. The cluster group added the project to the cluster plan and allocated funding. The cluster group enlisted the support of the health co-ordinator to organise the project. The headteacher in each school ensured that all school staff were aware of the rationale for the project and that everyone involved was aware of their responsibilities, including making space and resources available to those delivering the programme.

Ethos
The secondary school created a welcoming atmosphere for the range of different young people and adults using the venue during the main event. Positive relationships were encouraged between different age groups, between different educational establishments and between professional groups. The messages on alcohol promoted positive use of leisure time.

Partnership working
A number of specialist agencies were involved in working with teaching

staff to provide the programme. These included community police officers, voluntary organisations, a drama company, a school nurse, an
educational psychologist, alternative therapists and local health care co-
operative staff.

Environment
A display of the pupils' artwork was mounted along with information on
how support with alcohol issues could be accessed locally. Work was
undertaken in group sizes appropriate to the task.

Curriculum, learning and teaching
Lessons from the *Exploring Alcohol* pack were used in the Primary 7
Personal, Social and Health Education (PSHE) programme in the weeks
leading up to the event. Specialist agencies were made aware of the
curriculum content so that they could contextualise their contributions.
The Primary 7 visit was extended to create space for the programme.
The pupils worked in mixed groups, moving around workshops offered
by external contributors.

Staff health and well-being
Teacher training needs were addressed in advance of using the
Exploring Alcohol pack. Information on safe drinking and support for
alcohol issues was made available in the staffroom.

Participation of children, young people, family and community
Pupil councils were consulted in advance of the programme and evaluation was carried out afterwards to inform future planning. Senior
students acted as mentors, escorting primary pupils and helping with the
activities. A display toured the school, its associated primaries and
community venues.

The success of such programmes in the small number of ICS pilot schools
presented a challenge — with no increase in human resources, how could
other schools respond adequately to the Executive's directive on health
promoting schools? The solution lay in strategic planning; health
promoting schools came within the standards and quality framework and
supported by a quality improvement officer with the three health co-ordinators having an increasing role in staff development and consultation.

Although not included in the Scottish Executive directive on health
promoting schools, nurseries in East Renfrewshire perform very well in
health promotion and are included within the thematic standards and
quality review schedule. The challenge given to schools and to nurseries
is to identify where there may be gaps in service, and areas for development. A three-year development programme began in 2004, recognising

that the change towards health promoting status is a journey. Schools and nurseries are given the tools for self-assessment, and are encouraged to work with their partners to identify where they are on that journey. All schools and nurseries are externally assessed within a three year period by means of a thematic standards and quality review; those assessed as having very good practice are awarded 'Here's Health' status, and encouraged to celebrate their success with their community.

Conclusion

The ambitious nature of the ICS policy meant it was always unlikely that substantial impact would be demonstrable on all fronts within the three years of the pilot programme (August 1999 – June 2003), as the national evaluation from the University of London confirmed (SEED 2003). However, the evaluation team observed positive national trends, most of which involved the ICS projects acting as 'a catalyst for change and innovation'. More importantly, these observed changes lie at the heart of what the initiative is about: that is, they bring about more collaboration, and better services for vulnerable individuals and groups.

The East Renfrewshire experience confirms the national trend, but goes further. The changes experienced in this authority have been remarkable enough to gain commitment among many who were initially sceptical. They have been radical enough to change practice in mainstream services. Most importantly, they have built bridges between agencies and demonstrated that sometimes it is worth standing back from our furious activities to ask the question like the villager in the African tale, 'Why don't we work together to see if there is a better way of doing this?'

CHAPTER 3

JOINT WORKING IN SOUTH AYRSHIRE EARLY YEARS FORUM

Douglas Hutchison

Introduction

The bulk of an educational psychologist's work takes place within the context of statutory formal education. The advantage of this is that it provides at least a structure within which assessment and intervention can take place. At a very basic level there is normally a building where meetings, assessment, discussions and interventions can take place. In this context various workers can cross paths and occasionally bump into each other in the corridors or the classroom and relationships can be formed. The pre-school years from birth to 5 however are less formalised and there is no obvious 'building' where activities can take place. There is no obvious place where different agencies can come together to meet and focus upon the possible additional support needs of a baby or infant. In much of South Ayrshire therefore, as with many local authorities, the locus for such discussion, assessment and intervention becomes the Early Years Forum.

This chapter aims to describe an inter-agency approach to supporting pre-school children with additional support needs. This is done through the Early Years Forum which is a group of professionals concerned with addressing the needs of pre-school children within a geographical area determined by the catchment area of a secondary school. The Early Years Forum described in this chapter is one account of one such Forum in South Ayrshire. What follows then will be a description of the developments which led to the establishment of the Forum. There will also be a description of the types of issues addressed, along with two case studies which illustrate the way in which the Forum has operated recently. Following this will be an evaluation of the strengths and weaknesses of this way of working.

In addition to looking at the relative strengths of joint working there are other issues of relevance including the construction of the professionals' role and the relative power imbalance between parents on the one hand and the Early Years Forum as a group on the other. In addition to the powerlessness of parents there is an issue relating to consultation with children, whose voice is silent in this context.

South Ayrshire Council is situated in the south west of Scotland and covers an area of 422 square miles with a total population of 114,000 which has been stable for the last ten years. The authority contains a mixed rural and urban population with a mixture of advantaged and disadvantaged areas. Free school meal entitlement overall is slightly lower than the national average. The main towns include Ayr, Prestwick, Troon and Girvan. In addition there is an extensive rural area containing many small and remote villages. The council has responsibility for around 16,500 pupils in 45 primary and 9 secondary schools. Pre-school education takes place in 4 nurseries, 20 nursery classes and 12 partnership nurseries. The partnership nurseries are privately owned but have a partnership agreement with the authority. In 2000–01 all 3- and 4-year-olds took up a pre-school place compared to a national average of 96% and 87% respectively (HMIE, 2002).

Development of the Early Years Forum

Around September 1999, South Ayrshire Council produced a discussion paper entitled *Developing Educational Clusters into Partnership Arrangements that Support the Development of Community Learning* (South Ayrshire, 1999). While it is hardly a snappy title, the intention is clear. There are nine clusters in the authority based around the nine secondary schools and their associated primary schools. The intention is that these become the basic building blocks for developing area partnerships which support lifelong learning. It remains a core idea within the Council to have the cluster as central in co-ordinating and delivering educational services. This meant changes such as realigning support services to become part of a cluster rather than a centrally organised team. Link officers were established to connect the cluster with the central administration, cluster administration managers were employed and cluster pupil support co-ordinators appointed.

Along with this development in education, other services realigned their provision to match educational structures. Social work identified a link social worker for each cluster and community education was to be structured along similar lines. In turn it was straightforward for the psychological service to be structured around the cluster with an identified educational psychologist supporting each cluster or working jointly in some cases. The management of the cluster is carried out collaboratively by the head teachers with the link officer having a pastoral role aimed at improving communications between the cluster and the administrative centre.

A briefing paper from the director of education makes it clear that this development also includes pre-5 provision when he states that the expansion of pre-5 education, the full implementation of the 5–14 and Higher Still curricula, the promotion of inclusive education and the increasing emphasis on contributing to community learning plans underline the need for more effective co-ordination of all the educational activities within clusters of schools. (McCabe, 2000, p. 1)

Responsibility for the additional support needs of pre-school children had previously been held by a centralised multi-disciplinary group convened by the psychological service, the Pre-school Community Assessment Team or Prescat. Although in South Ayrshire, Prescat was considered to have been 'a highly successful child centred collaborative model with parents as equal partners and close interagency work' (Psychological Service, 2001, p. 1), several reasons led to a review of Prescat. Firstly, the development of the clusters raised issues for a centralised service. Secondly, Prescat tended to focus on children with complex needs who might have attended some form of special school, but, among other things, the Children Scotland Act (1995) had broadened the category of 'children in need'. Thirdly, there had been a significant increase in nursery places for 3- and 4-year-olds which meant that many of the issues previously dealt with by a central Prescat could be dealt with through the normal staged intervention process in a nursery establishment. As well as these developments, the Curriculum Framework 3–5 (SCCC, 1999) implied that individual planning should be embedded within curriculum planning in the nursery school or class. The result in South Ayrshire was the establishment of Early Years Forums.

In the past, Prescat meetings were held centrally in the psychological service building and were convened and in many ways 'owned' by the psychological service. For the reasons outlined above, this centralised system was changed to a number of local or cluster-based Early Years Forums. Five of the nine clusters have established an Early Years Forum. This probably reflects the reality that it may not be practical in all cases. As mentioned, several of the main centres of population are physically close to each other. This means in effect that the same health visitors, staff grade paediatrician and other health workers would be invited to discuss what in practice would be a small number of children. Given this, there has remained what has become known as a central Prescat for the schools where there is considerable overlap. For example there is only one denominational secondary school, which takes pupils from all over the authority. Its area would also cover the main centres of population and would involve duplication of staffing and so it does not currently operate an Early Years Forum. In practice therefore, where there have been advantages, clusters have moved to an Early Years Forum and where there would be considerable disadvantages the more central system remains in place.

Structure of the Early Years Forum

The Early Years Forum deals with an age range from birth to 5, or the start of compulsory education. Within this population the Forum is typically involved with children who are vulnerable for reasons of health, sensory, physical or communication difficulties. In addition the Forum aims to support children who are vulnerable for reasons of social, emotional or behavioural difficulties. The key targets for those involved would be social and educational inclusion.

The Early Years Forum comprises a core team of professionals from education, health and social work. This includes the staff grade paediatrician (Community Medical Officer), speech and language therapist, health visitors, social worker, educational psychologist and cluster pupil support co-ordinator. These members attend all meetings and then other individuals attend depending upon the additional support needs of the child concerned. Normally this extended team will include, very obviously, the parents and any support they wish to bring, staff from the nursery or school the child might attend and possibly staff from the authority's special school or unit if placement is being considered. Others from education might include sensory impairment staff from the visual impairment or hearing impairment team and the pre-school home visiting teacher. Additional health staff might include occupational therapists and physiotherapists, although more routinely reports and information come through the staff grade paediatrician. The staff grade paediatrician tends also to be the channel of information from child and adolescent mental health services.

The Forum meets four times a year, at which point new referrals are considered and current cases reviewed. Clearly there is frequent contact and activity between meetings, but these are the formal meetings where the main planning takes place and decisions are made. The dates for each session are set at the last meeting of each year and are usually in October, December, March and May. Referrals to the Early Years Forum can come from any of the core team or from a nursery or the parents of a child. In practice most referrals come from the staff grade paediatrician, health visitors or the educational psychologist.

The meeting itself is currently chaired by the educational psychologist and takes a standard format of reports from all involved including parents, followed by discussion and identification of any resources required. Action points are noted, with reports and minutes distributed after the meeting by the chairperson. Follow-up actions are the responsibility of the persons or services involved.

The following two case studies might help to illustrate some of the issues being addressed within the Early Years Forum.

Case study 1: Brian

Brian was referred to the Early Years Forum by the health visitor at age 3. Her concerns focused upon his development, which appeared to be slower than would be expected for a child of his age. His speech was immature and he tended to chew small objects he found lying around and he also chewed toilet paper and foam.

At the initial meeting when the referral was discussed, it was agreed that there should be assessment by the educational psychologist and the speech and language therapist. In addition the health visitor agreed to take on the role of key worker in relation to Brian and advise his mother on play and appropriate stimulating activities. The nursery Brian attended already had an individualised educational programme in place which focused on language development and appropriate social skills. These actions were agreed at the March meeting. Prior to the summer holidays, the health visitor and educational psychologist jointly sought out and secured Sure Start funding for support over the summer holiday period. The offer was made to find a private nursery place part time or find a child minder in order to offer a more stimulating environment for Brian and some respite for his mother. This offer of support over the summer was turned down by Brian's mother.

Concerns remained about Brian, and the case was reviewed at the December Early Years Forum. Assessment had been carried out by the speech and language therapist as well as the educational psychologist. A standardised assessment of receptive vocabulary carried out by the educational psychologist indicated a slight delay. However the speech and language therapist's assessment indicated that she had no major concerns about his receptive or expressive vocabulary and this was accepted as probably having more 'real life' validity than the formalised assessment of the educational psychologist. At this meeting the major issue became regular attendance at nursery. It was agreed by all, including Brian's mother, that he would benefit greatly from regular attendance. However, Brian's mother was experiencing significant family difficulties and was at times unable to bring Brian to nursery.

The recommendations from this meeting included that Brian's hearing should be checked again by the staff grade paediatrician and the health visitor should pursue the possibility of support in getting Brian to nursery in the morning. Brian lived within walking distance to the nursery. Following this meeting the health visitor and educational psychologist once again, jointly applied for Sure Start funding to employ someone to bring Brian to nursery each morning. While the funding was agreed it proved difficult to identify an individual willing to carry out this task who also had the necessary child protection clearance. Eventually an individual was found, but by then the funding had gone and it was not possible to employ the person who had offered to undertake the task. Brian is now due to start school and concerns remain about his progress. He will be monitored as part of the staged intervention review process.

Comment on Brian's case

While in some ways the outcomes were disappointing for Brian, the process was sound. The health visitor took a lead role in supporting the mother and her son and took responsibility on behalf of the Early Years Forum for trying to secure additional support for a young child whose mother was experiencing a period of difficult social circumstances. In the first instance resources were available but the offer of support was turned down by the mother and in the second instance the resource identified could not ultimately be funded. Although social work were not involved, it was still possible as a group to take action in the best interests of the child in a way which went further than the normal professional boundaries of any individual. The Early Years Forum provided a locus and empowered the health visitor and educational psychologist to carry out a function which might have otherwise been left to social work who in turn were absent due to staff shortages. During their involvement, the members of the Forum were satisfied that there were no child protection concerns. However, had this been the case these would have been referred to the social work department for further investigation.

Case study 2: Mark

Mark was first referred to the Early Years Forum by the staff grade paediatrician at age 2 years 6 months, due to a global developmental delay. At that point he had little speech, had not been walking for very long and his mother found his behaviour difficult to manage. The initial meeting agreed that a referral should be made to speech and language therapy, referral to the consultant community paediatrician who specialises in children with special needs, and the health visitor should consult with parents about appropriate support. It was also decided that a planning meeting should take place in the nursery, which Mark was due to start attending. The staff grade paediatrician would take the role of key worker in relation to the family.

At the following meeting of the Early Years Forum the medical assessment had taken place, which indicated that no significant barriers to progress seemed to exist but that delays were general. The speech and language therapist had also undertaken assessment and agreed that Mark would benefit from intervention. An individual support plan was formulated for Mark's starting nursery and referral would be made to the pre-school home visiting teacher with a view to supporting the parents in their management and stimulation of Mark. At this point it was agreed that further review would take place in the nursery and no longer within the Early Years Forum. However, the case had to be taken up again by the Forum as Mark's placement in the nursery began to appear untenable.

Review minutes from the nursery indicate that Mark would not separate from his mother and that his behaviour was a danger to himself and to other children. He would hit, slap and scratch the worker assigned to him and would run around with little control in the nursery. His time in nursery was cut to three hours and a Special Educational Needs Auxiliary employed to be with him for the hour a day he spent in nursery on a Monday to Wednesday. It was at this point that Mark's case came back to the Forum. For various reasons there appeared to be a lack of focus and co-ordination in relation to Mark's needs.

The Early Years Forum was able to look at the support which was in place, or rather which was not in place, and identify the gaps and occasions where there had been inadequate follow up. For example, the pre-school home visiting teacher had retired and had not been replaced so the mother felt as if she was struggling alone to manage Mark's behaviour. The headteacher of the nursery was absent on long term sick leave which meant in some ways the nursery staff were unsupported in a difficult situation. The Early Years Forum therefore decided that Mark needed to have one more attempt at maintaining a place in a mainstream nursery before consideration was given to an alternative placement. His time was increased to one hour a day each day of the week with additional hours in support given to the nursery. A temporary pre-school home visiting teacher had been appointed who would visit the mother to offer support at home. At this point outreach from the one special school in the authority was established and the possibility of future attendance at this school raised with the parents.

The following meeting involved staff from the nursery and from the special school, as well as Mark's father for the first time. Until now, Mark's mother had attended the meetings and indicated that his father was reluctant to admit that Mark was anything more than high spirited. This was a difficult meeting as it was clear that Mark's place at the local nursery could not be maintained. Little progress had been made in the time he had been attending. The suggestion of the meeting therefore was that he attend the special school nursery on a split placement basis with the local mainstream nursery. Mark's father was reluctant for him to attend a special school, so a visit was arranged to the school. Following this visit the father was less reluctant and a split placement between the local nursery and the special school nursery started. At present the intention is that Mark will start Primary 1 in the special school with a view to returning to his local school, initially on a split placement as the situation improves.

Comment on Mark's case

The reason for using this example is to illustrate the way in which the Early Years Forum, in spite of only meeting four times a year, was able to maintain focus and co-ordination when this appeared to be lacking elsewhere. This group was able to act effectively in resolving the situation when the mainstream nursery place was breaking down. The outcome at this point is that Mark is not in his local school, but he will at least be educated on a full time rather than a part time basis. This in turn reduces parental stress and may lead to improvement in the home situation. The intention remains that Mark should return to his local school when possible.

Strengths and development needs of the Early Years Forum

The one obvious strength of the Early Years Forum is that the group as a whole is stronger than the separate members who make up the group. This is strengthened further by the fact that regular meetings, with a focus on the needs of the children and families, have strengthened relationships between professionals. This makes communication outwith meetings easier. Under the previous centralised Prescat system there appeared to be more of an *ad hoc* feel to the meeting with less stability and permanence. This in turn meant that ownership remained with the psychologist and not with the combined services offered to children and families by social work, health and education. A stable group such as the Early Years Forum has more opportunity to take ownership together and determine the nature of the focus whether this is narrowly educational or more widely on the needs of pre-school children and their families. It may be in time that a more formal agreement between the services is required. Too much at present depends upon the goodwill and personality of the various participants. A further development over time might be a development plan for the Early Years Forum or the production of an annual report which summarises the activities of the Early Years Forum and which may also indicate some of the broader and common issues which relate cases. This would serve to move the agenda on from a traditional case by case focus to the wider issues affecting the children and their families.

At present however, a core group of members with local knowledge gives a greater sense of being grounded than a centralised Prescat which takes place in a town some distance away from local establishments and the home of the family. The health visitors in particular bring a wealth of knowledge which has the effect of rooting the Early Years Forum much more strongly in the local community. Among the professionals at least, there is a greater sense of ownership of the Early Years Forum and a strong focus on the children and family's needs. Once compulsory education starts, there is the danger that the needs of the establishment can, at times, play a significant role in the decision making process. Joint Assessment teams and Review meetings can be dominated, even numerically, by education staff. This can have the effect of influencing the agenda from being child centred to putting the wider needs of the institution first. Within the Early Years Forum the balance is more in favour of the child and family's needs. There is also a greater sense of equality amongst the professional groups represented rather than the proceedings being dominated by one service.

On the deficit side it remains the case that there is still not a sense of equality with parents. While every effort is made to include parents and it is likely that they will have seen each member of the Forum individually prior to the meeting, many still report feeling intimidated. This results in decisions being made and then later undermined by parents because, although they expressed satisfaction at the meeting, they later report that they did not feel they could say what they really felt at the meeting. This has happened on occasion but generally there is satisfaction with the outcomes of the meetings. A future development might be to ask the key worker to meet with the parent prior to the meeting and prepare a written report along similar lines to those presented by the professionals present. Equally more effort could go into canvassing the views of the child where appropriate. Once a child has language he or she should be able to express a view, even within the limitations available. Examples of good practice in this area exist such as the use of artwork, stories and role-play in the early years (Mortimer, 2004). At this stage we are very much at the start of the process of involving children. With children and young people, perhaps the process is as important as the outcome, and by asking their views it might be that they begin to develop a sense of agency. If their views are consistently ignored however, or asked for and then ignored, the effect might not be so positive. Clearly this is an area which needs attention and which may benefit from specific targets or being articulated more clearly in a development plan. While the ideal would be partnership with parents, at this stage a first step would be involvement which could be considered a step before partnership.

Another particular difficulty has been the involvement of social work. In the past year no representative from social work has been present at any of the meetings. Clearly in times of staffing difficulties a service has to prioritise where provision will be made. It is difficult to speculate on how different the service offered to families might have been, but it would be fair to guess that it might have been more complete. One positive side effect of the absence of social work has been the willingness of the members of the Early Years Forum to work together in ways which transcend the normal professional boundaries to try to address the needs of a child or family. One example mentioned earlier was the attempt to secure funding from Sure Start to help with a summer placement or additional childminding. Another example was support in applying for Disability Living Allowance and linking with the Princess Royal Trust South Ayrshire Young Carers who supported individuals in completing Disability Living Allowance forms.

Conclusion

This brief description of inter-agency working in the Early Years Forum has made no great claims nor does it make any reference to the learned literature. It is one person's experience of inter-agency working in the Early Years' sector in one part of South Ayrshire. Hopefully it is clear that this has largely been a positive experience, which has also been considered reasonably effective when compared to other attempts at inter-agency working. This perception of being a positive and relatively effective experience can partly be explained by the view that all the members of the Early Years Forum are firmly focused on the needs of the child and family. They do not appear to be weighed down by some of the other issues which afflict inter-agency working at secondary school level for example.

At times the inter-agency equivalent at secondary level appears to suffer from being an extension of the school's disciplinary procedure and risks becoming part of the continuum of exclusion. At secondary level, the psychological service was involved in a joint training initiative with all the members of a Joint Assessment Team. This was an attempt to apply the principles of solution-focused approaches to the meetings. Similar initiatives in the Early Years Forum might take the Forum a step further in terms of professional development. A team initiative should have more to offer than the sum of its parts and the collective professional expertise. This might involve specific training which focuses on the inter-agency process itself. One small example of this would be solution-focused approaches to meetings.

A stronger focus on the concrete needs of the child has also kept to a minimum any sense of professional defensiveness. It was interesting during the past session when a letter was sent to all schools from the staff grade paediatrician's line management chastising inter-agency groups for overstepping their boundaries and making decisions which were rightly the preserve of the medical profession. The staff grade paediatrician in the Early Years Forum simply expressed bemusement and life continued as normal.

Changes in personnel over the coming session should show whether it has simply been down to chance that the current membership of the Forum have worked very well together or whether it is the case that the structure and ethos of the Early Years Forum have allowed the group to function effectively. To this end a development plan with specific targets determined by the group itself would be useful. An annual review might also help to articulate what the group considers effective practice and effective joint working. From this it might also be possible to clarify what was done better together compared to what might have been done equally effectively by individual professionals. It will also be interesting to see how possible developments such as an all Ayrshire integrated assessment framework for children in need will affect inter-agency working. Such developments should fit well into groups such as the Early Years Forum where there has already been reasonably effective joint working and good relationships established. Whatever happens in the future it has been clear that in the past session there has always been a genuine willingness to do whatever is necessary to make something happen that would be to the benefit of the child and family.

CHAPTER 4

WIDENING OPPORTUNITIES FOR DISABLED CHILDREN IN STIRLING: A VOLUNTARY BODY INITIATIVE

Sue Dumbleton

This chapter explores the nature of partnership in the provision of a service which is not part of traditional education, health or social work but which has complementary aims to these services. The chapter also aims to link the development of a voluntary organisation to the wider social and political climate in which it operates. Playplus (Stirling) Limited or Playplus is a voluntary organisation which supports disabled children, teenagers and young adults aged 5–25 in play, leisure and other social activities. Playplus operates in the Stirling Council area and works in partnership with a range of other bodies, particularly Stirling Council. Throughout its 16 years Playplus has had positive relationships with its local authority partners, despite the changes brought by local government reorganisation. The first relationships, when local government was organised on a two tier basis, were with Stirling District Council and Central Regional Council. Since local government reorganisation in 1996 Playplus has related to the unitary authority Stirling Council. Stirling Council was the first Scottish authority to organise services on the basis of an integrated Children's Service which has responsibility for children and families' social work services, schools and Early Years' provision, out of school care and play services. It also has integrated provision for adults through its Community Services.

The initial impetus for Playplus came from an informal group operating in a political climate in which local government had given legitimacy to the public funding of childcare. In mid-1980s Stirling, play, as a central aspect of children's lives, had gained political credibility and funding. While the United Nations Convention on the Rights of the Child was not adopted by the General Assembly of the UN until 20 November 1989, the matter of children's rights was considered important by Stirling District Council as it had in 1984 followed the example of the Greater London Council and taken 'the potentially electorally unpopular risk of setting up the Women's Committee' (Kane, 1990, p. 19).

After consultation with local groups, one of the committee's first acts was to set up, in January 1985, a childcare working group to consider services and support for parents and children. Among this group's achievements was successful lobbying for council support for childcare which led, in 1986, to the opening of a council-supported crèche for children aged 12 and under. The crèche proved immensely popular. It provided safe, stimulating and centrally-based childcare. Local authority support for play was cemented in 1988 with the appointment of Scotland's first council-employed play development officer. Play in Stirling had been accepted as a legitimate target for public funding.

The struggle, during the latter part of last century, of parent led groups to gain access to education and health services for disabled children is well documented (ENABLE, 2004; Capability Scotland, 2002; Oswin, 1998). However, play and leisure were not, at that time, considered legitimate aspects for professional intervention, and access to leisure pursuits was certainly not considered a right. By 1988 most children in Stirling could enjoy play and leisure of right and enjoy the opportunities available for creative play. But not all could — and a casual remark about the long summer holiday and the lack of opportunity for most disabled children to be apart from family carers provoked a more interesting question. Where were these children? Not in playgrounds, swimming pools, parks, summer activities alongside their non-disabled peers — in fact these children were largely invisible, except to their families.

Small scale, local research, undertaken in the early and mid 1980s and reported by *The Stirling Observer*, had indicated both the woeful state of most of Stirling's play areas and the difficulties faced by families with a disabled child.

> These playgrounds are mostly unappealing places . . . five of the ten had no seats, no shelter, no toilets, no litter bins and no drinking water . . . fairly dangerous to all children, they are potential death traps for the very young . . . climbing equipment . . . whose design and construction has caused a number of deaths and injuries. (*The Stirling Observer*, 25 November 1983, p. 4)
>
> Having a handicapped child has brought isolation and loneliness at times. Gradually, invitations to my friends' houses stopped as they found my child's behaviour too difficult to accept . . . I was frightened of losing friends by demanding too much of them. (*The Stirling Observer*, 11 January 1984, p. 4)

Playplus was born from a chance remark made in a group of people sitting round a kitchen table. The chance remark linked what had seemed like separate issues. If public play areas were unattractive, unappealing and dangerous for non-disabled children, what of those who had additional support needs? And if the parents of disabled children faced isolation and loneliness, and clearly could not use such public play spaces as existed, a need to find a way of improving one to mitigate the other emerged.

Once the question — 'Where *are* these children?' — had been asked it was impossible to ignore. Round the table were people who worked with disabled children in a professional capacity and parents of disabled children — some were both. Why had none of them asked the question before? Perhaps, at least in the case of the parents, because the constant fight for statutory services identified by Beresford (1995) sapped their energies to the extent that they had none left to fight for something that was not the focus of organised intervention by service-providers.

For professional service-providers, the political context of children's play in Stirling as a public issue made its extension to include children with additional support needs seem logical. For while the newly-established Shoppers' Crèche encouraged the parents of disabled children to use its services by operating in a proactively inclusive way there was otherwise a lack of inclusive, staffed play opportunities. The need for Playplus had been identified.

A steering group was formed in the spring of 1988 to organise a 2-week summer playscheme for 10 disabled children and their siblings. This playscheme operated from school premises. A local special school for disabled children provided a building, which was physically accessible to all children. The school also had its own wheelchair-accessible minibus, which the organisers used to provide transport. Teachers from the school, well aware of the potential for social isolation for their pupils, endorsed the scheme and facilitated contact between the organisers and parents. Funding for this initial activity was minimal and came from a Central Regional Council fund — the New Deal for Disabled People. Funding in kind through the use of premises and transport also came from the Regional Council.

For some of the children involved, this was the first time they had experienced the sort of summer activity that most children take for granted. Children were well supported and safe, but were encouraged to make choices and take risks to create satisfying and stimulating play. Children who might otherwise have been at home for the 7 or 8 weeks of the summer holiday with no contact with children other than a sibling delighted in the company of their school friends and others. Siblings of the disabled children met others — enduring friendships were formed. Again for the first time, some parents experienced not only a break from caring but a sense of their child being positively welcomed and valued for him or herself rather than a 'problem' to be 'managed'. The feeling of acceptance was as important as the break. Trusting relationships between families and Playplus began to grow. Families will not use services that are unreliable or disorganised and building this trust was an important aspect of Playplus's first year. After the successful first venture, and the positive feedback from parents, children and professional staff, a quest for more substantial funding to continue the work began.

The women involved with Playplus saw possibilities for developing support to more children and at different times of the year. But even to recreate the initial 2-week playscheme meant that partner agencies had to be found. From the outset Playplus was committed to providing support to children to minimise the effects of disability and for this reason could not provide them on its own. Partnerships with other agencies are the means by which as normal a life as possible can be achieved for children and young people whose needs fall outwith the norm. For Playplus, the positive political climate and, particularly, the existence of the play development officer were crucial. The presence of a council officer gave the project legitimacy with professionals and funders and facilitated the early interagency working — such as the use of school premises — on which the continued development of the organisation has depended. This officer assumed a supporting and advisory function on the Management Board, and maintained clear communication between the organisation and the Council.

By 1990, when existing, but sometimes unco-ordinated, playschemes in the Stirling area came under the remit of the play development officer, the Playplus–Local Authority partnership formalised its joint working to develop an inclusive approach to all Council run play facilities. This partnership has meant that, almost from its inception, Playplus has not organised separate or special play opportunities for children aged under 12 but has been able to make use of existing facilities. The existence of Council funded play opportunities ensured that there was a structure with which the voluntary organisation could work to support access to social opportunities for all children. It also made it easy to seek funding from the local authority. Council support for play gave an important message about the validity of Playplus's aims.

In the late 1980s and early 90s the local authority, along with other bodies, funded Playplus through a number of departmental budgets — initially on the basis of 'one off' grants. While this funding enabled the group to formalise its provision and appoint paid staff to co-ordinate and provide a range of social activities, the early development of the Playplus service was on a somewhat *ad hoc* basis. These Council grants, for example, had outcomes calculated in terms of 'child hours' with no stipulation about the allocation of hours to individual children. Although Playplus was proactive in publicising its services it could not reach every disabled child in the Council area. Many children who received the service did so if they had families, teachers, health visitors, social workers or friends who knew about Playplus and could facilitate contact. Supportive of the aims of the organisation, and willing to contribute to funding, the Council made no requirements about outcomes matching individual need.

The management of the organisation, by this time a registered charity, was undertaken by a Board which comprised parents and professionals, such as speech and language therapists and health visitors. The link with the local authority was the play development officer whose advisory role gradually assumed a monitoring function as the Council made larger and more formal grants to Playplus. Staffing steadily increased with the increase in the number of families accessing Playplus support. Core staff, employed on a full or part time basis, co-ordinated support while sessional staff worked directly with the children. Apart from the Management Board, Playplus does not rely on volunteers for its work. An early decision was made to pay staff to undertake this complex work — one which still stands although volunteers are also welcomed.

Local Government reorganisation in 1996 resulted in the creation of a Stirling Council which assumed the responsibilities of the former Regional and District Councils. Fortunately for the development of Playplus, Stirling Council continued to regard play as a public concern through its Children's Services which provide:

> a wide range of play provision including the maintenance and development of public play areas, holiday playschemes and summer schools, special events and play projects, crèche facilities and a mobile service using the superbus and playvans . . . (Stirling Council, 2004)

In Stirling, play as a responsibility of the local authority is formalised through the Play Services section of Children's Services. Play opportunities are provided for children aged 5–12 throughout the Stirling Council area and it is with Play Services that Playplus has had its most fruitful and practical association in its work with young children. Building on its earlier work, disabled children aged 5–12 are supported in Council run play opportunities so that services are available to all children. Collaboration between local authority and Playplus staff to support individual children has worked well because of shared values and long term shared experiences — including shared in-house training. Training is regularly provided in a range of disability related matters and also in awareness of the impact of disability and barriers to accessing services. Because of the integrated nature of play provision and support, this training is of equal benefit to Council and Playplus staff. The ethos both of Playplus and Play Services is very child centred with choice as a key aspect of all activities. The non-statutory nature of the Council's play provision means that the legislative requirements attached to other council services do not impact on support for children's leisure activities. Positive and enduring relationships between Council employees and Playplus staff, particularly the presence on the Board of Management of a trusted Council officer, facilitated collaboration and ensured that Council run play opportunities for children were truly inclusive. Any child requiring additional support to access, for example, a playscheme or outdoor activity would be supported by Playplus staff working alongside the Council's team of playworkers. Playplus became well known, and was seen as a vital support for many families and children.

While inter-agency working with the Council's Play Services was well developed, a similar relationship with Children's Services, social work and schools took longer. There was, for example, until 2000, no dedicated team providing social work support to disabled children and their families. Without a partner agency, it is difficult to work collaboratively and although individual social workers and teachers knew about Playplus there was no formal mechanism for inter-agency work. However, two new developments led to a changed relationship with local authority schools and social work services. Firstly, the introduction of legislative requirements to provide services to disabled children and their families in particular (Children (Scotland) Act 1995) and disabled people generally (Disability Discrimination Act 1995) gave a further boost to the funding that the local authority was providing to Playplus. The Children (Scotland) Act 1995 makes specific reference to children 'with, or affected by, disability', defining them as 'children in need'. Local authorities are required to design services to minimise the effects of disability on a child and to give disabled children 'the opportunity to lead lives which are as normal as possible'. Although 'normality' can be contested, the law also makes specific reference to the requirement to provide after school and holiday care, services which, by the introduction of the law in 1997, Playplus was well able to provide. Individual social workers began to fund Playplus to support disabled children in established out of school provision, though on a rather piecemeal basis. For the families involved there were two benefits: children's social opportunities were increased and a natural break was created for parents and carers.

At this time the corollary of support to children — a break from caring for families — was formally recognised. In 2000 the Scottish Executive made available to local authorities money to fund support for carers. This money had to be spent in partnership with the voluntary sector. Stirling Council invested some of its Carers' Strategy money in Playplus to extend its provision to meet the needs of family carers as well as of disabled children.

In 2002 a new collaborative venture began with the launch of the Changing Children's Services Fund. This Scottish Executive initiative was designed to tackle child poverty and deprivation. Despite the passage of time since the local research that provided the impetus for Playplus, the Scottish Executive had discovered, through national research, that

> feedback from families with children with a disability or special educational needs shows that we have much room for improvement. Agencies often make separate, apparently unconnected, assessments of need and deliver support in a disjointed way (Scottish Executive, 2001b, section 11)

and was determined to tackle this through services with a 'preventative focus, providing support which make children and parents better able to deal with difficulties and to maximise opportunities available to them' (Scottish Executive, 2001b, section 15).

It was the emphasis on *prevention* that precipitated the most significant shift in Playplus's relationship with its local authority partners. In 2002/03 Stirling Council increased its funding allocation to Playplus by more than 50%. This increase came from the Council's share of the Changing Children's Services Fund and ensured that Playplus moved from being possibly available to children, but with no commitment or obligation to provide a particular level of service, to an entitlement model — which was designed to 'prevent' some children from needing a formal social work assessment. The provision of a supported social life, providing both child and family carers with positive experiences, was assumed to 'minimise the effects of disability' to the extent that some children and families would require no further, or reduced, social work services. For the first time, the importance of this aspect of children's lives as an entitlement, not a bonus, had been formally recognised and funded. Now, schools and social work services, the local authority agencies in closest contact with disabled children and their families had a shared target for involving young people in Playplus activities. Active promotion of Playplus by teachers and social workers at this time led to an almost 50% increase in the number of families involved during 2002. With the guaranteed provision of an entitlement of support sessions Playplus was contracted to provide an essential service on behalf of the local authority. For children and young people who need more than the basic entitlement, Playplus can be contracted as part of a care package and charge the local authority for these extra personalised services, for example the administration of drugs so that a child can participate in the Brownies.

This funding development has meant a move to greater accountability for the organisation. The outcomes of the service are no longer measured in 'child hours' but in provision and uptake of each child's entitlement to support. Playplus's target is to work with 90% of the disabled children aged 5–19 in the Stirling Council area, and the local authority shares the responsibility to inform families of the service. So, for example, there is dialogue between Playplus staff, social workers, headteachers and educational psychologists to ensure that families are well informed and that children receive the service. This greater accountability has also 'bought' for funders a place on the Management Board. Whereas the play development officer used to be the sole Council representative, there is now also the senior social worker for children with disabilities and other local authority staff. Inter-agency collaboration works well in an authority where non-statutory play opportunities are provided by its own services and statutory obligations under the Children (Scotland) Act are contracted out to Playplus. Developments in the wider world of social care have also impacted on Playplus which is registered with the Care Commission as a support service and is inspected against the relevant care standards.

As a way of involving colleagues in schools in its provision, Playplus runs a lunchtime club one day per week in one of Stirling's high schools. This is open to all S1 and 2 pupils and is aimed at supporting pupils both from the separate supported learning classes and the mainstream school. This club has proved very popular, and not just with the disabled students. Not all high school students enjoy unstructured free time at breaks so the provision of computers, dance mats, games and lively young staff once a week has appealed to a range of pupils. This club has met the aim of providing support for young people to access leisure and social opportunities, but the extent to which it contributes to the inclusion of disabled young people is less clear. Merely placing disabled children in mainstream classrooms does not automatically ensure that they will be well supported (Allan *et al.*, 1995; Connors and Stalker, 2002). Playplus recognises that children and young people are not necessarily included in their communities by placing them in mainstream play or leisure opportunities with support staff, even in their schools where they are potentially mixing with non disabled pupils every day.

Playplus's response to this has been to make a bid for funds to facilitate Circles of Friends with disabled children. Circles of Friends (sometimes called Circles of Support) started in Canada in the 1980s and comprise 'a group of people who meet together on a regular basis to help somebody (the "focus person") accomplish their personal goals in life' (Circles Network, 2004). This initiative will start where children's social lives usually start — in their schools — and will mean a further development of the partnership with Children's Services. A young person's Circle of Friends will positively include children in the partnership and will be wider than professional, inter-agency workers as, in the context of social inclusion, partnerships have to embrace as much of the whole community as possible. For children, this inevitably means other children. A worker will facilitate children and staff of many agencies in a new sort of partnership in which the main responsibility for inclusion will rest with the local group, or circle, rather than a specialist 'befriender' or a specialist disability agency.

Changing Children's Services money also made available, for the first time, secure funding for teenagers' activities. Although young people who had passed the age for supported play in partnership with Play Services had, in the past, continued to receive some support this had been on an occasional and uncertain basis. Formally 'youth services' were part of Community Services, not Children's Services. This made the forging of working relationships more complicated, but as a voluntary organisation Playplus was in a position to challenge departmental boundaries and work across services. Although much slower to develop, a relationship with the Council's youth team is emerging.

Changing attitudes, and policies, in adult services have helped this cross service work. A major Scottish Executive review of learning disability services, *The Same as You?* (2000) reported that '[People with learning disabilities] need to use public facilities more alongside non-disabled people, with less segregated sessions, events, shows and activities' (Scottish Executive, 2000, section 37).

These findings were, perhaps, not surprising in the context of contemporary Scottish research which provided evidence of social isolation amongst disabled adults (Riddell *et al.*, 2001). They echoed what young people and families knew anyway.

Feedback from service-users (Playplus, 1999/2000) indicated very high levels of satisfaction amongst children, young people and their families but that for many the approach of the nineteenth birthday was a source of some concern. As one parent noted, 'to go from getting a lot out of Playplus to nothing at all [will be] quite a let down'. As the young people who were associated with Playplus grew up and became too old to benefit from the support it could offer, stories of isolation and loss of friendships was began to emerge. At school leaving age, for example, many disabled children lost contact with their school friends. At a time of change in their lives, young people with the greatest need for support to maintain friendships were losing the support on which they had come to rely.

Guidance issued by the Scottish Executive Health Department reminded local authorities that, in implementing the 29 recommendations of *The Same as You?*,

> The independent sector is a key partner for the implementation of 'The same as you?'. In providing a significant proportion of services for people with learning disabilities, the voluntary and private sectors can make a valuable contribution to service planning and delivery. (Scottish Executive Health Department, 2004)

In response to this, Stirling Council Community Services has part-funded Playplus to develop a service for young people aged 18–25: 'The Bank' project. 'The Bank' grew from a small group of parents whose children had been involved with Playplus but who were reaching the upper age limit of its responsibilities. Apart from there being no adult services equivalent of the Council's Play Services with which a natural partnership could be forged, a desire for a different approach was expressed at consultative events facilitated by Playplus — Getting More from Life — with young adults in 2002 and 2003. These lively events captured the views of around 20 young adults through the use of video recording, discussion, art and music. Like most young adults, young disabled people want a social life that is separate from their parents, they want to sustain existing relationships and make new ones. They want to make use of the facilities on offer in their communities and they want to be able to relax with their friends. In fact, they aspire to an ordinary social life.

An ordinary social life is what 'The Bank' aims to support. The basis of 'The Bank' project, while not unique to Playplus, is new to most of the young people involved. A number of 'support hours' is available to each service-user, exchangeable for support at the request of the young person or his or her family or advocate. This puts the onus for requesting support to participate in social activities more firmly onto the service-user and moves away from the concept of organised leisure which is more appropriate to children. It also ensures that the diverse needs of this group of young adults can be met. For, as with so many other services, there can be a danger of assuming that activities that are valued by the majority are of equal value to all (Baxter *et al.*, 1993). As the parent of one young person who accesses support from 'The Bank' said, 'Not everyone wants to do what most people want to do' (personal communication).

The experience of establishing Playplus undoubtedly helped the development of 'The Bank'. Relationships with the local authority were long established, and the prospect of approaching the Council for funding was neither daunting nor unusual. Less than four years after the parent-led group started to plan for an adult equivalent of Playplus, 'The Bank' project has a full time paid co-ordinator, a number of sessional support staff and a cohort of 20 young adults on its books. Stirling Council Community Services now formally recognises 'The Bank' as a service with which it can contract to buy support hours to supplement individual care packages. This aligns with Children's Services arrangement with Playplus and validates the importance of a rich and fulfilling social life for disabled young adults as well as for children.

What has been learned from the experience of Playplus over the past 16 years? Firstly, its original aim of offering high quality social experiences to disabled children and young people still holds good. Despite legislative imperatives and service developments, the social lives of disabled young people generally remain impoverished compared with those of their non-disabled peers. For example, in 2003 Capability Scotland published *A Survey of Childhood Disability and Poverty* under the sub-title *Nobody Ever Wants To Play With Me*. It includes many quotes from disabled teenagers, including the title. It concludes:

> Many disabled children have few friends outside school and as teenagers they spend disproportionate amounts of their time in adult company . . . The lack of social opportunities simply reinforces the isolation of disabled young people on the margins of society. Our 1 in 4 poll shows that social injustice manifests itself in many ways for families living with disability.

Current research (Sharma and Dowling, 2004) indicates a continuing UK-wide dearth of social opportunities for disabled children and young people. Families in Stirling continue to contact Playplus, and numbers of children and young people supported continues to grow with now well over 200 young people involved. There is always a number of families waiting anxiously for their child's fifth birthday, the age at which Playplus support can begin. Sixteen years after it was established, Playplus is still needed and Playplus still needs partners to achieve its aims.

Postscript

Late in 2004, in the period between writing and publication, Playplus was renamed PLUS. PLUS has retained the name Playplus for its work with 5–12 year-olds. Its work with 12–19 year-olds is called 12.19 and 'The Bank' works with 18–25 year-olds. Up-to-date information can be found at www.plus-stirling.org.uk.

CHAPTER 5

DEVELOPING INTEGRATED MENTAL HEALTH SERVICES FOR CHILDREN AND YOUNG PEOPLE IN MORAY

Chris Wiles

Introduction

Moray is situated in the north of Scotland, lying between Aberdeen and the rest of Grampian to the east and Inverness and the Highlands to the west. It has a population of almost 90,000, of which almost 21,000 (approx. 24%) are under 18 years old. Moray covers a considerable and diverse geographical area, ranging from the mountains of the Cairngorms to the south and the Moray Firth coastline to the north. The area is famed for its farming, forestry, fishing and the distilleries, which produce some of the finest malt whiskies in the world. More recently Moray has hosted a significant proportion of the Royal Air Force in its two airbases at Kinloss and Lossiemouth, and the oil industry employs large numbers from the area. Although some of the more traditional industries are in relative decline, the area is still economically and socially vibrant.

Moray Council was formed in 1996 following Local Government reorganisation. Prior to this, Grampian Regional Council held the strategic and operational lead for local authority services for children and young people in Moray. Since reorganisation Moray Council has had to come to terms not only with the transition to unitary authorities, but also the increasing local focus of the devolved Scottish Executive's policies and guidance. In 1997, Moray Council entered into a partnership with the voluntary sector to provide residential care and community support services. These partnerships not only led to several voluntary organisations having a significant presence in Moray, but also led to the beginning of increasingly inter-agency working for children and young people in need. Within the education sector, a variety of village and rural schools feed eight secondary schools and despite falling rolls in some areas, the New Community School development has created solid foundations for inter-agency working.

In 1996 when Moray Council came into being, the health service locally was contained within a single combined trust, Moray Health Services, which provided a range of community and acute services commissioned by the then Grampian Health Board. At this time the local authority and the health service were essentially co-terminous and worked relatively well together, particularly with regard to certain areas of need such as mental health, the elderly and people with a learning disability. In 1999 the NHS system was reorganised and health services across Grampian were contained within two Pan-Grampian Trusts: an acute service trust and a primary care and community services trust. The role of the Health Board also changed towards a more strategic role with greater focus and direction from the Scottish Executive. These changes meant that in Moray some of the continuity and senior management connection to the local authority was lost as well as local services within the locality being managed and directed by different parts of the wider health system, all based further away from the area. In April 2004, following the Scottish Executive's *Partnership for Care* White Paper (2003), the health system is in the process of further reorganisation. This has led to a move away from the two Pan-Grampian Trusts, to a combination of Community Health Partnerships co-terminous with the local authorities. These moves are designed to enhance the local delivery of services whilst creating better strategic and management for the service as a whole at the Grampian level.

The history lesson is important as it highlights the tremendous amount of structural reorganisation over recent times, which does impact on service delivery in many ways. It also raises issues about ownership of both strategic direction and provision of services and the complex systemic issues which dictate, to an extent, the response children and young people in need receive. Another factor, the importance of which cannot be overlooked, is the development of the devolved Scottish Executive and its considerable activity in terms of legislation, policy and guidance. Over the last few years both local authority and health services have been faced with a variety of directives and policies, many of which are innovative and important but, nonetheless, complex and time-consuming to roll out, and the range of direction is often conflictual and fragmented in practice.

Mental health services for children and young people in Moray

In Moray there have been Child and Adolescent Mental Health Services (CAMHS) to some degree for the last twenty years or so, but it was 1986 before a full time psychiatrist was appointed, based in Moray. The team developed with the addition of two nurses and a part-time social worker seconded from the local authority. In 1997 clinical psychology sessions were added, and the team began to operate in a more multi-disciplinary way. At this time, the service was felt by most other agencies, particularly within education, to be inaccessible, uncommunicative and unhelpful with long waiting times and limited presence within the community.

In 1998 the team decided to address this and redefined itself as a child and adolescent mental health service as opposed to a psychiatry team. It was renamed the Rowan Centre. This decision was an attempt to reduce the stigma for young people and their families, but was also a statement about the joint approach and the focus on young people and their needs, by association with a traditional folk song about wishing in vain to be young again.

Currently, the team consists of psychiatry, clinical psychology, nursing and social work clinicians. It now works as a multi-disciplinary, organisational unit for receiving referrals either assessing and/or intervening together or operating by discipline or specialism where appropriate. A defining conceptual framework for the service is an understanding of systemic theory and practice. This drive came from staff with experience of working within systemic family therapy services but also the practical experience of working with young people who were connected to many other agencies and helpers within and external to their families. It was felt that supporting young people directly could be enhanced by indirectly supporting others within their systems. This approach became the foundation for working within the wider community of services for young people, influencing opinion about mental health and exploring the links between all the agencies to support young people's mental health.

The systems approach has helped to build the commitment of the team in the context of the complex and changing environment and the different personalities of the team. Despite pressures from increasing demand, clinical work was undertaken jointly in order to learn about each other's skills and abilities and establish best practice with regard to assessment and interventions. A programme of service development was given protected time, allowing staff to be released to engage with external agencies and also to explore wider aspects of current service provision. Working groups were established around specific clinical concerns and the day-to-day responsibilities and tasks of running the team were shared.

Progress was co-ordinated through a schedule of team days, where discussion and team building activities took place. The mixture of personalities, paces and an ability to contain differences of opinion, and even at times to value and celebrate differences, has led to considerable development. In many ways the team has become more multi-disciplinary in its approach to the task of understanding the concerns and worries which bring young people and their families to the clinic. The operational aspects of the service are shared and not led by a specific discipline, but are defined by individual skills and enthusiasms based on shared ideals and trust in each other.

The move, however, from an inaccessible service on the hill to a more connected and focused team has led to an unprecedented rise in referral rates with numbers increasing by approximately 50% in 3 years. This is not only an indication of the unmet need within the community, but shows the response from those working with young people who previously had nowhere to take their concerns about the mental health of the young people in their charge. During the time when a systemic approach was being enhanced within the team and referrals were increasing, the team introduced a triage system to help cope with the rising demand. This also reflected the team's experience of increasing case complexity and the reality of increased multi-agency involvement in many of the cases being managed.

The triage system involved families and older young people themselves completing descriptive and screening questionnaires prior to being offered an appointment. Permission slips were also signed allowing for pre-appointment contact with any other agencies involved. The triage clinics were given protected time, and clinicians from all disciplines within the team paired up to provide a screening assessment session, the purpose of which was to identify a clear statement of the difficulties and a plan for further enquiry or support. The triage system and the increasing connection with other agencies began to develop into a more shared approach and ownership of mental health within children and young people's services. The team also began to offer other agencies an opportunity to have consultation about a young person without the need for a full referral to the team. 'Did not attend' rates and the response time from point of referral were significantly reduced.

A successful bid to the Health Improvement Fund led to a variety of audit and service development projects across with other agencies. The realities of increasing working together on a case-by-case basis, alongside the service development commitment and a significant range of Scottish Executive policy and guidance, evidenced a shifting culture within Moray around CAMHS. However, in a Grampian context CAMHS had been split across two Pan-Grampian trusts with different organisational and management structures. Some of the services were within the child health structures of the Acute Trust whilst the rest were within the mental health structures of the Primary Care Trust. This split led to a relatively weakened strategic drive across Grampian with minimal service provision and no development funds for CAMHS.

Locally becoming more involved with other agencies led to better working together, more strategic discussion but also to more time being taken up with supporting these links and in resolving the wide ranging conflicts which arise when closer working relationships are developing. Unlike the clinical team where the goals of multi-disciplinary working were clear and committed to, this was not always the experience of joining up at a multi-agency level, where the realities of other agencies' internal conflicts and issues and pressures often dictated their response to joining up activity. This was complicated further in Moray by the local authority's relationship with the voluntary sector, which had led to more services but also to considerable blurring of roles and confusions around ownership and leadership within the community. In an audit during this time, only about a third of the cases within the team did not have another agency involved, with another third having multiple involvements (i.e. more than five). In some cases as many as ten workers were directly connected to a case and practicalities such as confidentiality issues, the timings and venues for meetings as well as more 'soft' issues such as value base and training experience were often complicated further by the numbers of staff involved.

New Community Schools were already challenging the cultures and activities within schools and communities around integrated, inter-agency working. Trying to get CAMHS on the map during these complex and fast moving times required the type of resource, space and focus which was incredibly difficult to maintain, especially whilst the level of enquiry and referral continued to rise. The issue of ownership of mental health issues was complex and challenging for all. Within education, the sense that mental health was another policy drive taking staff further from core education tasks often led to resistance, although some were able to recognise mental health as a core function of education itself. This variability of understanding was evident in staff across all agencies and reflected our own struggle with how to prioritise and organise to have maximum impact on the greatest need. Small victories slowly opened up wider communication. These connections allowed for staff in the community to feel engaged with staff from the service in ways which meant the perceived sense that we held magical solutions which we were unwilling to share was challenged and more realistic collaborations established.

One of the consequences for the team of this level of change was an intense pressure to develop at great pace that left limited opportunities for reflection. The need to hang on to protected team time increased the more change the system created. In addition, the emotional impact of the clinical work itself cannot be forgotten. One of the consequences of more inter-agency connections is the need to help others recognise the potential effects on them as they support young people with complex and painful histories in challenging situations which can be extremely difficult to change. This often led to discussions and reflections on other professionals' frustrations, limits and boundaries and the need for support and supervision for them in the same way we were trying to hold onto for ourselves. In conjunction with a mental health promotion consultant, we provided guidance staff from schools with a workshop on exploring definitions and concepts of mental health. These workshops invariably resulted in discussion about staff support, given complex demands from their service as well as from young people directly. The relationship and support experiences within this process cannot be understated as they led to the most significant changes in understanding and practice.

Integrating services for children and young people in Moray

A feature of the development of mental health services has been the context of partnership working in Moray. The partnerships described above between the local authority and the voluntary sector and also the focus for New Community Schools are evidence for the types of processes that define integration. These processes require considerable effort to maintain and can be vulnerable to the impact of individual personalities and also the difficulties in co-ordinating efforts and directing resources to the areas of greatest need. At various points in the last ten years the local authority and the health services have been closely linked in terms of their identity and aims. Both organisational structures have historically been a smaller part of a wider Grampian structure, and this shared history does allow for a shared sense of local identity and perhaps even a drive to develop and deliver locally. The size of the area and its structures also means that there are fairly flat management lines and that the strategy and planning are closely related to the experience on the ground.

As the partnerships have developed there has emerged a need for a system of planning and organising shared activity. Within the local authority itself the social work and education departments had begun to meet formally on a regular basis to respond to the strategic and policy demands of the Council, but also to allow for a shared forum for discussing and planning for individual children in need. The voluntary sector became part of these forums, as they had become agents of the delivery of the social work task. The health sector on the other hand was harder to engage with in a meaningful way, partly because of the structures within health and also because of the small size of certain elements of health service resource. However, due to the efforts of a number of individuals from all sectors, a more consistent health presence began to emerge.

The expanding forum had a variety of Scottish Executive multi-agency directives to respond to and two multi-agency integrated funding streams in particular helped to secure further commitment to formalising such a network approach. The Changing Children's Services Fund which followed the Scottish Executive's *For Scotland's Children* report (2001c), and the second phase of the New Community Schools funds became the catalysts for more collective and integrative service development. The two funds were effectively combined and the total resource used to support the existing infrastructure and to fund specific projects evidencing innovative joint working.

The process of consulting, creating, negotiating and agreeing what to fund led to further discussion about formalising the group which had began to co-ordinate and discuss the wider strategic issues the funding had opened up. The outcome of this process and further consultation days, facilitated by an independent consultant, led to the formation of the For Moray's Children group (FMC). The FMC established its parameters from the *For Scotland's Children* report and agreed to continue to collectively develop services and share the responsibility for the whole process.

The initial outcome of the FMC was a variety of projects including the construction of the Local Community Networks. These networks brought together all agencies within an area school group's catchment area and allowed for a restructuring of the social work teams to match these local area units. Project officers were appointed to each area to co-ordinate integrative practice, stimulate joint working and also provide the infrastructure for a planning meeting system for young people within the area who required multi-agency approaches and resources to support their difficulties.

The FMC's development related well to the Community Planning process, which was emerging as an important focal point for both the local authority and the health service. The next Children's Services Plan could then be written as a single system plan which could represent and feed into each of the services' action plans and a variety of other bigger plans covering specific areas such as the Joint Health Improvement Plan. To meet this objective the FMC commissioned a series of working groups on, for example, mental health, children with a disability, youth crime, child protection, early years, substance misuse and looked after children.

Each of the groups was asked to identify current provision, develop an action plan, and establish a multi-agency reference group involving young people and their carers as much as possible. The groups were then to explore single service approaches and to discuss various crosscutting issues such as age transitions, rural issues, agency communication and service-user and carer involvement. The groups have had to deal with a range of challenges including the complex tasks of chairing the groups, getting a balanced mix of participants from management and staff across the agencies with knowledge and experience of the issue, getting good venues to meet in and communicating more widely about the discussions and seeking support or other views. The groups are yet to complete the task but the Scottish Executive has since issued new guidance about the aims of the Children's Service Plan, which indicates the importance of universal service issues as well as those directed at children in need. This will mean that the outcomes of the working groups will need to be wide and focused on early identification and resource management.

Crucially, another agreed task of the FMC was to improve communication and widen the debate about children's issues both within the community of services targeted at children and young people and the wider population. A website has been developed to do just that and each member of the FMC network has a responsibility to communicate with staff within their organisation about the activity of the group with all being encouraged to contribute. The FMC held a conference for staff across all services called 'Getting It Together For Moray's Children', which allowed for consultation on progress and also for networking across the whole system. A follow up conference called 'Getting It Together Again', in November 2004, allowed for feedback and wider discussion about the development of the children's services plan but was also a celebration and demonstration of integrated practice across children and young people's services.

Mental health becomes everybody's business

As the For Moray's Children group was developing as described, the task of enhancing the services to support the mental health needs of children and young people in Moray continued. The enhancement centred on two processes. The first was the opportunity for discussion locally with other services and ultimately bid for new resource to the Changing Children's Services Fund. The other process was happening at a Grampian level, where CAMHS in both trusts began to develop better links and work in a more cohesive strategic direction. The Health Improvement Fund had allowed for some audit and development work to be done in all of the services and the sharing of this work created a realisation of the poor overall resource and the relative lack of support for the services as a whole within the health system. Representatives from all of the specialist CAMHS and their managers formed a group to construct a development plan which created an agenda for the future and a costed implementation plan.

Despite the plan being supported by the newly appointed Child Health Commissioner within the Health Board, it has not led to any new resource at this point due to the intense financial pressure within the NHS system in Grampian. However, the process of writing the plan had been somewhat cathartic and had also resulted in the establishment of an Operational Management Group to continue the work of improving resources, but also to start working on the agenda the plan had highlighted. This has already led to some significant changes to the relationships across Grampian and also the support for improving the integration of services at a local level, although there is, without a doubt, a very long way to go.

The NHS Scotland report (2003) on CAMH aimed to identify ways of better addressing the mental health needs of children and young people, through the promotion of positive mental health, activity to prevent mental health difficulties and when and how to provide help for those children and young people who are experiencing mental health problems. It carried out its enquiry from published research, and a process of surveys, seminars and consultations with children, young people and those who care for them and work with them. The report made a series of recommendations around integrating the promotion of positive mental health with increased focus on prevention as well as improved systems of care. The report focused on the need for the 'mainstreaming' of mental health, essentially suggesting that mental health became everybody's business.

It also gave a useful context for the discussion within Moray and helped create the climate for a bid for a new and integrative service, CALM (Consultation, Advice, Liaison in Moray) from the Changing Children's Services fund. CALM was developed to promote enhanced opportunities for partnership working through direct support to agencies in Moray whose primary task with young people was not mental health. These agencies comprise professionals and staff who work within children's services but who do not perform a specifically defined mental health role, including education and social work staff, staff in voluntary and social care organisations, and health service staff, including therapists, in both primary and secondary care paediatric services.

The project aimed to provide workers and managers within these agencies with opportunities for consultation, liaison and support around specific child and adolescent mental health issues within their workloads. CALM also aimed to provide agencies with a fast and responsive initial mental health assessment, which could involve a combination of discussion with agency staff and direct contact with children and their families. The outcome of these assessments could lead to further comprehensive assessment at the Rowan Centre, or through another agency, and to more comprehensive and cohesive packages of support for the child and their family. One outcome would be the maximising of the capacity of the most specialist services, allowing for better targeting of this level of support and the availability of this service for partner agencies. In addition, it was envisaged that these increased opportunities for joint understanding, management and working across the agencies would lead to an increased sense of ownership of these issues and, in practice, staff would have an accessible point of contact to raise concerns about specific children or more general issues about mental health.

The experience of CALM

One year into the project, progress had been such that a further two years of funding has been secured. Making the specialist service more visible and accessible has been, on the whole, a hugely significant shift. It has led to more joint working and to a wider appreciation and understanding of mental health issues within young people's services. It has also led to a significant improvement in the recognition of previously unidentified or unmet need. This has led to a justifiable increase in referrals to the specialist services, but also a more accessible and relevant range of supports for services working with mental health difficulties within their workloads.

Some examples of the activity include: training days for guidance staff, health visitors and residential care staff about mental health issues for young people; a protected time for consultation meetings for those involved in complex cases including teaching staff; workshops for young people in schools about mental health in conjunction with health promoting school staff; audit work and development of responses to school refusal in conjunction with educational psychology, paediatric staff and schools; increased direct contact from guidance staff about specific young people and an audit of the mental health needs of looked after children leading to establishment of protected consultation time with care staff.

The project however, has also been a major challenge for the staff within the specialist team at the Rowan Centre, who were stretched even further to get the project up and running. It is fair to say that the response to the project was very positive on the whole. However, not all of the staff across the services shared the same hopes and ideals for positive mental health and a significant amount of stigma was encountered. The project also took us right into the heart of a wide range of issues within and across services which, despite not necessarily being directly about mental health issues, definitely impacted upon their management. One particularly disappointing experience was the relatively poor uptake of training about mental health issues. Reviewing the experience has led us to re-focus activity, in negotiation with the managers of other services, for the next phase of the project.

The ongoing resource will allow the continuation of the inter-agency agenda, with more dialogue, discussion and planning to ensure that services accept and develop their responses to mental health and create the mainstreaming approach. In years to come it is hoped that this will lead to better opportunities for young people to develop emotional resilience, inter-personal skills, problem solving approaches and coping strengths as standard aims, rather than by chance.

One significant issue is the mental health of those supporting young people, many of whom are overwhelmed with a variety of operational, professional, organisational and personal struggles which makes it very hard to role-model what we are hoping for our young people. A clear example of this comes from our experience of providing mental health workshops in schools where, in myth-busting discussions about mental health, pupils are always able to identify their teachers who they feel are stressed, distressed or struggling in some other way with their mental health. Better relationships with the young people we are charged with supporting may not only allow us to help them to learn good survival skills but may also allow us to learn from them about our own realities as well.

'What do we need to stop playing at this and to do it properly?'

This question is one that we have continued to come back to in our attempts to develop our service and also to support others in their response to young people's mental health needs. If mental health is really to become everybody's business there is a lot that needs to be done.

Clearly, the total resource question remains and the whole process requires considerable investment if we are to reach the hopes and aims which have been identified. The use of joint-agency short term funding may well generate activity but it continues to be risky in relation to building sensible and sustainable resources which are viable from a work-force perspective. The aims in themselves, however, require a significant amount of airing and sharing to become accepted as widely held objectives within an overwhelmed, fragmented and generally un-coordinated system of services for children and young people, where everyone feels under pressure. If we truly value young people and their potential then we must value the services that support them in tangible ways beyond strategy and rhetoric.

Champions are needed not only for young people but also for their services. Young people themselves must be central to these expressions and consultations and campaigning. Thus far, much is said about involving young people, and indeed their carers, in how services are shaped; however, little has been achieved in making real experience count in planning terms. Asking young people about what they need and want, or even being able to capture their interest in the questions, can be extremely difficult. Youthstart, and more recently Dialogue Youth and similar enterprises, require ongoing development to ensure that young people's voices are heard loudly and have impact on the thinking, the activity and its planning. Communication and meaningful consultation with the families and carers of young people are just as problematic, although the developing recognition of carers' rights and support systems should in time lead to improved opportunities for dialogue. Ongoing and focused discussion across agencies must also be a priority, not only in dusty meeting rooms, but also in schools, social work departments, family centres and GPs' waiting rooms. Knowledge about each other's agencies is key and consideration is being given locally about job-shadowing experiences. Also important to enhance integrative practice are clear and simple service directories, increased use of web-sites and email communication, clearer and more focused cascading of information, and ongoing consultations and debates.

For this to happen on the frontline, the strategic focus needs to improve, ensuring that the right levels of ownership and management across agencies and operational units exist. The complex equations of size, scale and need require space and time to manage. We need the ongoing national drive but also local leadership and enthusiasm, some of which is enhanced by new resource and the hope that it can bring. The shared hopes of developing integrated responses to the mental health needs of young people require lots more discussion with lots of people lots of times, with new resources, new thinking and new structures. The size of this task cannot be understated, and the resilience, patience, interpersonal and coping skills we hope for our young people will be required by us all if we are to get there.

CHAPTER 6

SPACE FOR GROWTH

Ann Glaister and Bob Glaister

Children are at the heart of the developments described in this book. Policy developers and practitioners are signing up to the notion that providing children's services which benefit all children in a holistic way is the desired outcome of the transitions that are under way. Perhaps we are seeing indications of the changes in mind set that Cohen suggests are necessary (p. 12). The focus of the book and of the case studies has been on the experience of practitioners involved in trying to move things forward. What has it meant for them? How does it connect up with what has gone before? What are the challenges and the benefits, as they see it, to the ways in which they can work?

Researchers have quite reasonably wondered whether the involvement of 'a range of professional agencies, parents and the voluntary sector, make complicated decisions easier or easy decisions more complicated' (Riddell and Tett, 2001, p. 1) and have pointed to the challenges inherent in policy developments designed to address such broad agendas as social inclusion in the context of battles over such things as budgets, ideologies, reporting lines and differential legislative frameworks (e.g. Tett *et al.*, 2001, p. 105).

This final chapter, however, draws out lessons from the case studies to illustrate how some progress is nonetheless being made towards developing working models of integrated services for children and reflects on these accounts in the context of a wider literature. *For Scotland's Children* (2001c) proposes that approaches tailored to the particular circumstances of different localities should allow a variety of models to emerge and this is indeed what seems to be happening. Each account is unique and contextualised, presenting a rich array of challenges and achievements.

We suggested in the Introduction that this final chapter would consider what is being learned about inter-agency working in the context of these case studies. What we have tried to do is to consider first the issues in common that seem to arise and then to reflect on what might be done to facilitate progress. A review of the case study accounts yields a greater wealth of ideas and detail than we can treat fairly in this single chapter. Our strategy has been to read them again and again asking ourselves, 'What were the common issues that seemed to play a part in these integrative developments?' The case study authors may use different terminology, have different priorities and perspectives and emphasise different aspects of their experience, but the four interweaving issues identified below represent the factors that have emerged for us.

- capitalising on synergies between local developments and national policy drivers;
- working across the spectrum from universal to targeted provision;
- building communication and trust across professional, institutional and agency boundaries;
- evolving community-based partnerships with parents and young people.

The case studies illustrate the development of quite new service structures and styles and often quite startling and complex growth curves. The 'upstreaming' allegory recounted by Mackenzie (p. 13) captures the aspiration of many practitioners. Practitioners share a sense that doing more of the same is not really tenable as the workload increases and there is no diminution of pressure in sight. Yet facing the prospect of developing a different approach to try to prevent the escalating problem raises huge challenges in the short to medium term. This, of course, is recognised explicitly in the provision of the Changing Children's Services funding designed to support the necessary bulge of work involved in instituting change. Despite this, practitioners have to learn on their feet, often quite literally, and have little time to stop and think about what is happening and why. This final chapter tries to create that opportunity for reflection, exploring and learning from the accounts that have been presented here.

Capitalising on synergies between local developments and national policy drivers

It is almost a truism to assert that national policy developments with funding streams attached can have an enormous impact upon local activity, though the short term nature of such funding may bring problems in its wake. Each of the first three Action Plan recommendations in *For Scotland's Children*, for example, mention resource issues as central to success (Scottish Executive, 2001c, p. 107). It is no surprise, therefore, that the case study authors acknowledge such funding as facilitating initiatives. Dumbleton notes the advances which followed the Children (Scotland) Act (1995) and the Changing Children's Services Fund (2002), even in an authority which already had a significant record in children's services (see, for example Moss and Petrie's account of Stirling's achievements, 2002, pp. 168–9). One development (Mackenzie, p. 13) arose directly from New Community Schools funding and Mackenzie observes that they were also able to capitalise on the addition of Sure

Start funding to secure and enhance their promotion of family learning by developing a new family learning team with a dedicated family learning manager. Hutchison, too (p. 26–7), describes how national shifts in Early Years and Special Needs framing and resourcing influenced the South Ayrshire development of a cluster approach to an Early Years Forum.

The apparent clarity of such links disguises the fact that someone has to recognise the local value and relevance of the funds, has to have a vision and has to be creative. There is seldom a direct one-to-one relationship between policy and what happens on the ground. Indeed in this instance, the conceptualisation of children's services explicitly recognises that local arrangements and priorities will have a role in determining just how ideas are put into practice (Scottish Executive, 2001c, p. 77). Nor is there an intention to start from scratch, wiping out what has gone before. Changes will be driven forward, nonetheless, some of them involving major restructuring.

Cohen's chapter tells the story of an evolutionary process of policy development, particularly in relation to Early Years' thinking, harnessing and amending legislation over the years. What is particularly interesting in this account is the sense of policy as a living, breathing process, engaging people's hearts and minds in a struggle to achieve and deliver on a vision. This chimes with other writers' accounts of the policy process. Davies (2000), for example, proposes the concept of 'provenance' of a policy, enabling an examination of stakeholder thinking to be brought into the frame along with 'acknowledgement of the multiple and messy character of the policy process' (Davies, 2000, p. 221). There are multiple stakeholders involved in this ongoing process, including not least, the elected politicians, the employing agencies and the professionals responsible for delivering the services and the not to be overlooked service-users, children, young people and their families who stand to gain or lose from what is achieved. It is not just a case of putting in place a policy and expecting practitioners to comply.

There are fascinating glimpses of the recognition points where synergies become apparent between aspirations on the ground and the existence of new frameworks and funding flows at policy level. The links are always easier to see retrospectively. At the outset, round the kitchen table, Dumbleton and her friends and colleagues had no notion that their thoughts on the lack of supported play opportunities might ultimately connect with mainstream funding flows in support of statutory provision. It took a sustained effort of creative imagining to, not only hold on to, develop and begin to find ways to implement their idea in partnership with the local authority, but also to be continually open to spotting the opportunities for tying this to policy initiatives, legislation and funding.

Wiles' initial concern was to deliver a more effective and accessible service. His thinking led him towards increased levels of communication with other agencies. Moving already towards greater degrees of networking and collaboration, he and others could then see the opportunities available and how they might together bid for funds. In Moray, they were ultimately able to bring together two funding streams to maximise impact — New Community Schools funding and Changing Children's Services funds.

Building communication and trust across professional,
institutional and agency divides

Not surprisingly, a key theme to emerge is the importance of developing shared values and experiences. Dumbleton, for example suggests that, 'Collaboration between local authority and Playplus staff . . . has worked well because of shared values and long term shared experiences' (p. 40). McCulloch *et al.* (2004), considering inter-professional collaboration in the context of New Community Schools in Scotland, found 'trust' to be perceived as an important indicator of effective collaboration. They found it to be 'often a by-product of personal connections and friendships' (p. 141). For all of the case study authors here, this is a central issue. To forge a unified, national children's service in any meaningful way requires a transcending of boundaries between professions, institutions and agencies, but there appear to be no golden rules other than the need to recognise that it takes time and opportunity to learn to understand each other, to work together and to build trust. Joined-up working is influenced greatly by the compatibility of the remits of the different agencies. It is not insignificant, in this regard, to note that all current local authorities have been in place only since 1996 and the NHS seems to be in permanent reorganisation. Both of these groups of public services are designed to meet local needs, but without their geographical remits having any clear relation to each other.

Wiles outlines graphically the complexities faced in Moray where local authority and NHS structures are not co-terminous, but for Wiles, the starting point had been with inter-professional working *within* the child and adolescent mental health service team. They needed to clarify their own objectives and ways of working; to develop better understandings of each other's strengths and approaches; and to develop more effective decision making, case review and allocation processes and support mechanisms within the team. As a part of that process wider issues were addressed and the image and identity of a service, still seen as child psychiatry, was raised. Re-naming their location The Rowan Centre softened the prior perception of this as a medical service. A more neutral and localised identity perhaps also conveyed a capacity to operate more independently, despite their structural home still within the Grampian Region Health Trust. They were then better placed and more clearly seen as an appropriate entity for consultation when it came to discussions with other agencies and institutions — local authorities, social service departments, schools.

This moved them into the more complex sphere of developing collaborative approaches with colleagues, not only from other professional backgrounds, but also with accountability to different agencies and with different concerns and priorities. Initial attempts to offer workshops to teachers to develop some more shared understandings of mental health issues were welcomed, but few signed up in practice. From the teachers' perspective, the Rowan Centre was there to lift some pressure from the school by providing targeted intervention and support for children and young people with a range of worrying mental health problems. To suggest that they themselves could learn more about such problems and how to understand them may well have felt threatening.

Perhaps this was an indication that some further alignment of priorities and pressure points had to be undertaken first. McCulloch *et al.* (2004) concluded that 'Inter-professional collaboration may be seen as a threat rather than a benefit, especially when core aspects of people's professional competence may be questioned' (p. 142).

A New Community School, on the face of it, provides an easier location for collaboration to grow in new ways across old boundaries. People work within one institution. Their management structures and the value base and priorities will be to a considerable extent in line with each other, if not the same, even if terms and conditions of employment may be different. Different agency and professional identities may remain as tensions and support and supervision may lie elsewhere, but as working colleagues they have considerable opportunities to learn from each other. Mackenzie describes the depute head coming to recognise the year round nature of the social work task (p. 19):

> I still get frustrated when the social worker takes holiday during the term, but I now remember that when we all leave at the end of June, the children's need may be greater and family stress increases — someone needs to be there to bridge that gap.

Such collaborative working can lead to a widening of agendas. The work of the New Community School remains primarily educationally focused but there is a shift from a mind-set in which social work and health professionals are seen as adjuncts to teaching priorities to one in which they engage in setting the priorities.

Hutchison, on the other hand, hints at the work that has still to be done when he suggests that the integrated focus of the Early Years Forum on the child with additional support needs is less recognisable in the formal school sector, where the wider needs of the institution can appear to be dominant. In secondary school, he suggests, the process risks becoming part of 'the continuum of exclusion' as it operates almost as 'an extension of the school's disciplinary procedure' (p. 34). The forum seems to create a successful local focus but results in other boundary issues when it comes to linking more broadly. However, the planks are in place for further integration via link officers with the central administration, link social workers, dedicated educational psychologists and community education workers.

The extent to which the New Community School solution still results in a gravitational pull towards an over-emphasis on school education and curriculum rather than the wider aspects of community life, mental health and wellbeing remains to be seen. Sammons *et al.* (2003) had noted a tendency for New Community Schools to be 'viewed as an education initiative by partners and that considerable effort was required to encourage joint ownership and pooling of resources' (p. iv). McCulloch *et al.* (2004) noted that 'from the perspective of the different schools studied, effective collaboration stems from the capacity of the partners to add value to the schools' efforts' (p. 140). Hutchison's description of non-educational staff as 'support staff' is, therefore, not surprising or unusual and the references here and elsewhere to parents providing support for their children's learning, while perfectly healthy and beneficial, again reflects an assumption that the primary shared task in children's services remains an educational one.

One further boundary that deserves mention is that between statutory and voluntary services. There can be serious tensions here and there are concerns that alignment of children's services may reduce the creative opportunities available to voluntary agencies. Not so in the example here. A striking aspect of Dumbleton's account was the symbiotic nature of the relationship between social services and Playplus. Not only were they able directly to help the local authority deliver on its statutory duty; not only did their objectives map well onto Stirling's reorganised Children's Services, but they also found themselves in harmonious accord in terms of their outlook and value base. Her reference, quoted earlier, to 'shared values and long term shared experiences' reflects a longer term period of growth than other case studies here. It also may reflect to some extent the establishment of shared training opportunities. With time, such mutual trust makes planning and co-ordination much easier, especially when it happily coincides with the availability of funding. Nonetheless, challenges had to be faced and new partnerships formed with youth services and with schools. The ultimate shift towards provision for adults is a reminder that coherent children's services require careful attention to be given this frontier. Holistic children grow into holistic adults and attention has to be paid to this boundary. The Scottish Executive departmental challenge of where to 'put' lifelong learning as a concept in the context of children's services already serves as a reminder of this issue.

Working across the spectrum from universal to targeted activities

Health and Education are universal services with substantial targeted or needs-led elements. Complex issues are bound up in this, as Cohen suggests, not just in relation to where the responsibilities should rest and the impact such decisions will have. The proposal for additional specialist resource to be brought to bear competes inevitably with a view that universal services should be more flexible in their capacity to meet needs. As Wilkinson points out in discussing the new agenda in early education, 'It is difficult to reconcile the principle of targeting with the principle of universality' (Wilkinson, 2003, p. 76). Wilkinson's focus is with vulnerable children, but the exclusion of 'troublesome' children from school is the prime example at the forefront of teachers' minds, with feelings running high as to where the line should be drawn. Hutchison describes the tensions around such discussions (p. 32). There may be a difference of perception and vision at play here between '*child*-centredness' for targeted services, and something more akin to '*children*-centredness' for universal services.

Such concepts are not, of course, absolute. Local authority education departments retain legal responsibility for the education of excluded children and considerable flexibility does indeed exist both within and outwith schools to provide targeted help in response to need in order to maintain supported access to the curriculum for individual children in difficulty for a multiplicity of reasons. Health authorities have a different set of responsibilities in relation to children. While they will have universal targets and expectations, in relation for example to inoculation and screening programmes and will hope that their health visitors will see as much as they can of babies and toddlers, particularly where there are concerns about their development or safety, this does not constitute a statutory, universal service in the same way as education. Like education, however, primary health care does provide an unstigmatised first port of call for many. Targeted services, for example social work or mental health, are by their nature brought into the picture where there are identified needs and concerns, bringing with them the pathologising implication of something being wrong. The change in title described by Wiles, from the child psychiatry team to the Rowan Centre, is a clear attempt to get around this problem.

Mackenzie's account of the circus skills project and the Alcohol Concern venture suggests exciting and creative ventures that drew together a multiplicity of service inputs within a universal setting, including services which might usually be seen as specialist. The position of the health workers and social workers in the school made the potential for impact far greater. The 'courageous decision' to appoint social workers to the school was significant in reducing the potential stigma attached and certainly eased the complexity of inter-agency consultation and planning.

To return to the upstreaming analogy, collaboration in the prevention of problems can ease life all round. To some extent flexible and effective universal services can 'catch' or prevent problems before they occur, but expertise and time inputs from specialists are also likely to be important.

Hutchison draws attention to the advantages of co-ordinating such expertise to support smooth decision making and planning in order to arrive at the best outcomes for children and families. Dumbleton's specialist play workers can ease not only play opportunities but also social inclusion through integrated provision for disabled children and young people. Mackenzie is undoubtedly concerned with exclusion issues but has shown that a decrease in exclusion can be achieved in parallel rather than in conflict with improved outcomes.

Understanding can flow from talking across these frontiers — from a case to a class focus, perhaps, and vice versa. Mackenzie's social worker, for example, comes to realise why one child missing a day a week of school is so problematic and needs to be responded to. 'I had not appreciated before how devastating an 80% attendance rate is for a child's education not just for that child but for the teaching of the whole class' (p. 19). Teachers, on the other hand, may begin to prioritise an understanding of mental health problems as a way of facilitating their work with all children and may be given the time and support in future to participate in Wiles' training workshops.

Lastly, while the Moray study focuses on the trials and tribulations of co-ordinating targeted mental health services for young people, it recognises that, if such provision is going to shift upstream, 'ongoing discussion across agencies must also be a priority, not only in dusty meeting rooms, but in schools, social work departments, family centres and GPs' waiting rooms' (p. 57). The physical location of meetings and provision carries significant messages about the universality of the issues.

Evolving community-based partnerships with parents and young people

Inter-professional and inter-agency working is challenge enough and it is not surprising that evaluations frequently find there is still a long way to go when it comes to working in partnership with young people, families and the community. Sammons *et al.* (2003) for example, in their review of the pilot phase of New Community Schools in Scotland, found few initiatives aimed at engaging parents in dialogue about their children's learning and few instances of systematic consultation with communities. Similarly Baron *et al.* (2003) in their report on the Glasgow Learning Communities suggest that, despite good progress on other fronts, the initiative has 'not yet substantially addressed the relationships between school, pupils, parents and community'. They argue that 'Recognition needs to be given to parents and community interests as "stakeholders" in the educative process' (Executive summary, p. 2). Is it possible in these case studies to see movement occurring away from the polarization implied in the 'them and us' of service-providers and service-users towards the point where all in the community are seen as potential participants?

Dumbleton's account starts in the community as a largely parent-led initiative powerfully influenced and informed by the direct experiences and needs of the growing young people and their families. Their starting point is as the key stakeholders and they retain their position. Their primary concern is not, however, with Baron's 'educative process', but with the wider issues of social inclusion beyond school agendas and beyond school gates. There is also an awareness of changing needs and wishes with age and of individuality: 'Not everyone wants to do what most people want to do' (p. 45). Lively consultation events designed to gather young people's views using video recording, discussion, art and music become part of the partnership and community engagement process itself rather than just a means to an end. The shift from thinking in terms of service or facility to an allocation of hours to be drawn down as desired also seems to reflect a new balance in the relationship with greater autonomy and respect afforded to the young people and their families.

Hutchison, looking from the other end of the telescope, expresses concerns about the relative power imbalance which, he feels, still exists for parents:

> While every effort is made to include the parents . . . many still report feeling intimidated . . . a future development might be to ask the key worker to meet with the parents prior to the meeting and prepare a written report along similar lines to those presented by the professionals present. (p. 33)

Such shifts in attitude and practice are hard to achieve and the gradients and distinctions between engaging parents in a pre-defined, professionally-controlled process, for example, compared with building partnerships where agendas and priorities are open to debate, are not well understood. Different styles of partnership will be appropriate in different circumstances: for example, involvement at the level of planning services will be different from addressing the needs of one's own individual child — and, as Hutchison indicates, professionals have to be sensitive to such distinctions.

Mackenzie also sees parental involvement as a core issue. She sees the shift from involving parents as educators to a broader involvement in terms of the wider community, as the key challenge to traditional practice. This is no longer about them being corralled into school activities, mixing paint etc., 'but affirms parents as educators and values *family involvement in learning over parental involvement in school*' (p. 16, our emphasis). The engagement of families and the wider community in lifelong learning becomes the focus rather than the experience of children as pupils within the school gates. There are echoes here of the Playplus agenda, although it is *learning* here that replaces *education* as the central concern rather than a broader concept of social inclusion through play and other activities. Mackenzie describes parents, however, as seeming more comfortable about seeking a range of appropriate support.

The For Moray's Children group see their task of building partnership at community level in similarly broad terms, setting up a web-site to widen the debate. Wiles suggests, though, that much is said about it but little achieved. Capturing the interest of young people can be difficult and meaningful consultation with carers can be equally problematic. Champions are undoubtedly needed to take the partnership agenda forward. Consultation with young people in Moray, however, has already led to interesting observations about *professionals'* mental health issues. Wiles points to

> workshops in schools where in myth-busting discussions about mental health, pupils are always able to identify those teachers who they feel are stressed, distressed or struggling in some other way with their mental health (p. 56).

The 'them' and 'us' split between service-users and providers begins to spin on its axis. It is not only young people who may have the problems and the widening of perspectives and agendas in this way may be precisely what is needed to move forward.

Allan *et al.*'s (2004) research had focused on this axis as significant in trying to evaluate the impact of New Community Schools. These researchers had considered the schools as sites for the potential production of social capital in the wider community and saw the extent and nature of communication between professionals and the community as a key measure of success. This is not about professionals and services seeking to engage service-users and the wider community in their professionally defined activities. Rather it is about working *with* the community to recognise and address commonalities and differences in perspective and priority. Improving networking and communication between service-providers and service-users are, they suggest, essential, but difficult to achieve.

From services to spaces

We have asked our contributing authors to describe their experiences of inter-agency working. Their focus has therefore been on the ways in which the services they are involved in are working to recreate or restyle themselves. They are operating in complex, emotionally demanding and sophisticated services, struggling with changing policy environments and keeping provision going day-to-day in the teeth of significant re-structuring, forging new working relationships and developing new and shared agendas. What is striking is the degree of enthusiasm that shines through; the sense in which a shared commitment exists to meet the needs of children, young people and their families more effectively. Despite the difficulties, and the sense that there is still a long way to go, one can see the professionals' struggle to hold the children in the centre of the picture. We reflect here, in this final section, on what might be done to facilitate this developmental process.

When thinking about how society provides for children, we were very impressed by Moss and Petrie's book, *From Children's Services to Children's Spaces* (2002). They believe that the concept of children's services

> is bound up in a particular understanding of public provisions for children: a very instrumental and atomising notion . . . [with] . . . pre-determined and adult-defined outcomes. The concept of 'children's spaces' understands provisions as environments of many possibilities . . . some pre-determined, others not, some initiated by adults, others by children. (p. 9)

These spaces are not just physical, 'a setting for groups of children', but also social, cultural, discursive. The reconceptualisation adopts a different discourse to consider 'how children and their provisions may come to shape an uncertain future rather than being shaped for a predictable and pre-determined future' (p. 2).

We cannot here do justice to the richness of Moss and Petrie's contribution with regard to provisions for children, but it has rung chords with us as a useful way of reflecting on what is happening in terms of inter-agency and inter-professional working. They are speaking largely of public space in which children may encounter and negotiate with each other relatively freely: spaces in which children may *play*, unencumbered by adult expectations, guidance and restrictions; spaces which are all too rare today. They would exclude some of the spaces which have been our concern in this book — spaces arising within the purview of services such as schools, nurseries, youth clubs; spaces which rest largely on an adult perspective on where children should be heading, in terms of their learning, their behaviour, their suitability for subsequent employment, their safety, their success or otherwise in slotting into family and social relations. Moss and Petrie recognise that too often the here and now of childhood for its own sake is buried in favour of visions of what the child must become. Yet the here and now of childhood is also about growth and development, about striving and discovering, solving problems, stumbling upon new questions, learning from mistakes. And children will do this not only in free space, but also in classrooms, in day nurseries, in clinics, in clubs — almost anywhere in fact if they are given half a chance. We felt therefore that service-based professionals may adopt an orientation towards creating such space for children — freedom for intellectual, emotional and social growth: a space for growth.

What became apparent from our case studies was that, in order to achieve this, professionals too need 'space for growth'. Moss and Petrie argue in fact for a new form of professional, in line with the European concept of the pedagogue (Moss and Petrie, 2002, pp. 145–6). The necessary breadth of understanding and skill required to provide appropriate, holistic support for children and families should be vested, they suggest, in one kind of person, rather than emerging from an attempt to achieve incremental change by pulling fragmented, existing services and professionals together under a new unified organisational structure. Policy in Scotland, and in England, however, has not taken this line (Scottish Executive, 2001c, p. 74).

There is abundant testimony from the literature that successful inter-agency collaboration and inter-professional working cannot be achieved overnight. As well as structural change with linked strategic funding, a serious commitment to appropriate training and staff development is needed (see, for example, recent comments from Stewart *et al.*, 2003, and Allan *et al.*, 2004), and our cases reveal some examples of the value of such formal processes. In terms of formal, qualifying and post-qualifying training, professional bodies have begun to address the need for inter-professional skills as an essential part of a core curriculum. This is true for nurses, social workers and increasingly for teachers too. An essential component of achieving Chartered Teacher status, for example, is the demonstration of a capacity to work with others, and Integrated Community Schools will increasingly require teachers to work across professional and agency boundaries. This is a significant shift for professional bodies from a tendency to focus on professional status and identity, heightening distinctiveness and difference, and protecting boundaries quite ferociously. The challenges of a future, in which shared curricula, shared training and even shared assessment feature in initial professional education, are just beginning to emerge.

In the meantime our case studies provide some more informal examples. Dumbleton points to the benefit of shared in-house training between Playplus and play services staff on a range of disability related matters. Hutchison proposes specific training focusing on the inter-agency process. Wiles talks of the value of job shadowing — 'Knowledge about each other's agencies is key and consideration is being given locally to job shadowing experiences' (p. 57). Allan, too, had quoted a welfare professional on the importance of shadowing:

> My feedback from the work shadowing is that generally people did not have a lot of knowledge about what other professionals did — where they were coming from, what their responsibilities were, where the limits to their responsibilities were. And the trust thing — I think there has been a fairly low level of trust across certain services, like teaching, social work, health visiting to some extent — and there have been huge gaps, like with clinical psychology and child psychiatry, where the knowledge base has been almost non-existent. People have been shocked to find out what social

workers actually do. They had no idea of the complexity. (Allan, 2004, p. 154)

Particularly interesting is Wiles' tribute (p. 49) to joint reflective time:

> A programme of service development was also given protected time allowing staff to be released to engage with external agencies and also to explore wider aspects of current service provision . . .

and there was a 'schedule of team days where discussion and team building activities took place'.

There will be a need for these structured opportunities and activities if professionals are to develop, but they also, like children, require to engage in creative processes of growth and development; they too have to strive and discover, solve problems, stumble upon new questions, learn from mistakes, especially in an environment where there is a broadening of agendas and an increasing focus on wider consultation and partnership. They will need an ever-widening space for growth as the agendas become less predetermined, the boundaries with the wider community are less rigid, the agentic space for young people is greater, and the power relations between service-providers and children, young people, their families and the communities in which they live are more balanced and operate with more mutual respect.

As the service-provider / service-user axis spins, maybe the next step is to stop thinking so much in terms of that polarising division at all. Perhaps the focus should be not so much on delineating new professional roles and inter-professional working as on reconceptualising space and opportunity for growth — for all participants, including children, families and the wider community. The framework for the implementation of integrated children's services may need to give more attention to providing such inclusive space.

What is to happen in this space? Is it anything more than just an obvious statement: that if people are to work together they will need some time to talk to each other? Undoubtedly, creating space for growth — for all — may depend on a number of things, of which protected space and time may be the first and most difficult essential to achieve. But opportunity for participative learning is about more than just being together in space and time. Comments emerging from our contributors connect with ideas explored elsewhere about the nature of the teamwork process, the way in which discourse can be attended to, ensuring that minority views are not marginalised and power imbalances are handled respectfully. Opie (2000) has described this as 'knowledge work'. Her book, based on research in New Zealand, offers a valuable, in depth analysis of what happens when teams and clients are working effectively. Working together is not, she suggests, about bringing together parallel sets of ideas for recycling, adding them up or seeing which wins out as the most powerful, nor is it to suppress disagreement or arrive at bland value statements with which no one can disagree. The process she describes is one of knowledge creation, in which the team works to 'reconstitute their knowledge' and to 'refashion their collective and individual knowledge of the client'. It requires 'trading in ambiguity and fluidity and the identification of alternative spaces that may be (temporarily) occupied and regarded not as oppositional but as augmentative' (p. 257).

Perhaps some of the developments described here contain the seeds of such knowledge work and of such opportunities. Creating a forum for discussion, holding consultative workshops, debating issues with young people, with parents, with other agency representatives — all these provide space for such knowledge work and 'augmentation' to occur. It creates the opportunity to develop insight into one's own position and perspective and to share that, but also to remain open to hearing and learning from others. This is not about winning and losing points or advocating one view over another. It involves learning to offer a perspective and to value others' contributions, as a part of an exploration in which all are involved.

Signing up to the principle of joined-up working in order to deliver a better deal *For Scotland's Children* is a good starting point, but the case studies reveal the complexity of moving in these directions. At every level there are significant challenges: a new and more integrative policy; commitment at national level to inter-agency working; professional body engagement with the need for training to address working with others as a central concern — each are hard to achieve and require ongoing endeavours. Achieving change, however, is not just about putting new structures and formal agreements in place. Professionals find themselves engaged in processes and relationships, which require them to find fundamentally new ways of thinking about what they do for, and with children. They must engage with other professionals, often from other agencies, to explore what outcomes are valued and to work together towards new, shared understandings. If children are seen as children (or perhaps as people) first, rather than pupils, for example, what does this mean for educationalists? Or what might 'child-centred' mean in the context of a targeted compared with a universal service, where 'children-centred' might be more accurate? Not only must they learn to work across these professional boundaries, however. They must also learn to work with young people, their families and the communities in which they live. They must ensure that community values and perspectives are heard and understood in relation to the well rehearsed, though often conflicting, views and priorities of professionals.

In Opie's terms this means engaging in knowledge creation, with the ambiguities and fluidity that necessarily entails. To achieve this requires something more than just formal restructuring, more than formal training and development opportunities. In Moss and Petrie's terms, we would argue that what is needed is space: space in which there can be freedom to explore new agendas, build new relationships and to tolerate uncertainty. If understanding is to be augmented, as Opie proposes, it may be necessary to stumble around a bit at first exploring the nature of the new spaces and positions which might be adopted in those spaces.

Setting the metaphors aside and returning to the case studies, we can see real examples of such spaces being sought after and sometimes created: Wiles' notion of 'joint reflective time'; Mackenzie's account of the development of the circus skills project; the Early Years Forum described by Hutchison; and both Dumbleton's and Wiles' accounts of different consultative sessions with young people. All of these have in common a sense of openness as to agendas and outcomes, a willingness to take risks and to work together towards something new. If inter-agency working is going to succeed in delivering joined-up working, particularly working which engages meaningfully with community and service-user agendas, then, we would argue, professionals will need protected time and space in which to grapple with new skills, new relationships and new thinking. The case studies attest to a great deal of work already under way, and a thriving commitment to achieve more, but support will be needed to ensure the necessary learning can take place. In the midst of demanding work schedules and pressing responsibilities, those striving to work together to provide space for children to thrive, will themselves need space for growth.

BIBLIOGRAPHY

Allan, J., Brown, S. and Riddell, S. (1995) *Special Educational Needs Provision in Mainstream and Special Schools in Scotland*, Interchange 38, Edinburgh: Scottish Office Education and Industry Department

Allan, J., Mannion, G. and Duffield, J. (2004) 'Premature evaluation? Measuring the impact of New Community Schools', *Scottish Educational Review*, Vol. 36, No. 2, pp. 145–58

Baron, S. (2001) 'New Scotland, New Labour, New Community Schools: new authoritarianism?', in Riddell and Tett (eds) (2001), pp. 87–104

Baron, S., Hall, S., Martin, M., McCreath, D., Roebuck, M., Schad, D. and Wilkinson, E. (2003) *The Learning Communities Initiative in Glasgow: Report to the Director of Education*, Glasgow: Faculty of Education, University of Glasgow. Available from URL www.scatprojects.org.uk/glasgowsummary.asp (accessed 1 October 2004)

Baxter, C. et al. (1990) *Double Discrimination: Issues and Services for People with Learning Difficulties from Black and Ethnic Minority Communities*, London: Kings Fund

Beresford, B. (1995) *Expert Opinions: A National Survey of Parents Caring for a Severely Disabled Child*, Bristol: The Policy Press

Bloomer, K. (2003) 'The local governance of education: a political perspective', in Bryce, T. and Humes, W. (eds) (2003) *Scottish Education*, Edinburgh: Edinburgh University Press, pp. 159–67

Capability Scotland (2002) *Capability Scotland – A Brief History*, Edinburgh: Capability Scotland

Capability Scotland (2003) *Childhood Disability and Poverty*, Edinburgh: Capability Scotland

Cavet, J. (1998) 'Leisure and friendship', in Robinson, C. and Stalker, K. (eds) (1998) *Growing Up With Disability*, London: Jessica Kingsley

Children in Scotland (1997) *1995 Children (Scotland) Act Information Pack Factsheet No. 4*, Edinburgh: Children in Scotland

Children in Scotland (2000) *Guide to the Standards in Scotland's schools etc. Act*, Edinburgh: Children in Scotland

Children in Scotland (2004) *Children in Scotland*, September 2004, p. 13

Circles Network 'Circles of Support', www.circlesnetwork.org.uk/circles
_of_support.htm (accessed 30 July 2004)

Cohen, B. (1998) *Children's Services: Time for a Fresh Approach?*
Edinburgh: Scottish Local Government Information Unit

Cohen, B. (2002) *Children in Europe*, Issue No. 3 Focus on . . . Scotland,
pp. 18–21

Cohen, B. (2003) 'Scotland's children and the new Parliament', *Children
and Society*, Vol. 17, pp. 236–46

Cohen, B. (2004) 'A Sure Start in Sweden', *Community Care*, 1–7 July
2004, pp. 36–7

Cohen, B., Moss, P., Petrie, P. and Wallace, J. (2004) *A New Deal for
Children?: Re-forming Education and Care in England, Scotland and
Sweden*, Bristol: The Policy Press

Coleman, P. (1998) *Parent, Student and Teacher Collaboration: The
Power of Three*, London: Sage

Connors, C. and Stalker, K. (2002) *Children's Experiences of Disability:
A Positive Outlook*, Interchange 75, Edinburgh: Scottish Executive
Education Department

Davies, C. (2000) 'Understanding the Policy Process', in Brechin, A.,
Brown, H. and Eby, M. A. (2000) *Critical Practice in Health and
Social Care*, London: Sage, in association with The Open University,
pp. 211–30

ENABLE (2004) *Far beyond Our Dreams*, Glasgow: ENABLE

Fullan, M. (1993) *Change Forces: Probing the Depths of Educational
Reform*, London: Falmer Press

Her Majesty's Inspectorate of Education (2000) *Alternatives to
Exclusion*, Edinburgh: HMIE

Her Majesty's Inspectorate of Education (2002) *Inspection Report on the
Education Function of South Ayrshire Council*, Edinburgh: HMSO

Kane, M. (1990) 'From inside the Council: local government women's
committees in the 80s', in Henderson, S. and Mackay, A. (eds) (1990)
Grit and Diamonds: Women in Scotland Making History 1980–1990,
Edinburgh: Stramullion Ltd and The Cauldron Collective

McCabe, M. (2000) *Report by the Director of Educational Services to the
Educational Services Committee of 3 Feb 2000: Developing
Educational Clusters*, Ayr: South Ayrshire Educational Services

McCulloch, K., Tett, L. and Crowther, J. (2004) 'New Community
Schools in Scotland: issues for inter-professional collaboration',
Scottish Educational Review, Vol. 36, No. 2, pp. 129–44

Mortimer, H. (2004) 'Hearing children's voices in the early years',
Support for Learning, Vol. 19, No. 4, pp. 169–74

Moss, P. and Petrie, P. (2002) *From Children's Services to Children's
Spaces*, London: RoutledgeFalmer

NHS Scotland (2003) *Needs Assessment Report on Child and Adolescent
Mental Health*, Edinburgh: Public Health Institute for Scotland.

Available from URL www.phis.org.uk/pdf.pl?file=publications/
CAMH1.pdf (accessed 1 May 2005)

OECD (Organisation for Economic Co-operation and Development)
(2001) *Starting Strong: Early Childhood Education and Care*, Paris:
OECD

Opie, A. (2000) *Thinking Teams: Thinking Clients*, New York: Columbia
University Press

Oswin, M. (1998) 'An historial perspective', in Robinson, C. and Stalker,
K. (eds) (1998) *Growing Up with Disability*, London: Jessica Kingsley

Penn, H. (2002) *Since Strathclyde*, Edinburgh: Children in Scotland

Playplus (1998) Annual Report, Stirling: Playplus

Playplus (1999/2000) Parent/Carer Questionnaire, Stirling: Playplus

Riddell, S. and Tett, L. (eds) (2001) *Education, Social Justice and Inter-
Agency Working: Joined-Up or Fractured Policy?*, London: Routledge

Sammons, P., Power, S., Elliot, K., Robertson, P., Campbell, C. and
Whitty, G. (2003) *New Community Schools in Scotland Final Report:
National Evaluation of the Pilot Phase*, London: Institute of
Education, University of London

Scottish Consultative Council on the Curriculum (1999) *A Curriculum
Framework for Children 3–5*, Dundee: SCCC

Scottish Education Department (1977) *Truancy and Indiscipline in
Scottish Schools*, Edinburgh: HMSO

Scottish Executive (2000) *The Same as You? A Review of Learning
Disability Services*, Edinburgh: Scottish Executive

Scottish Executive (2001a) *Better Behaviour, Better Learning*,
Edinburgh: Scottish Executive

Scottish Executive (2001b) *Changing Children's Services Fund
Consultation on Priority Objectives and Mechanisms for Allocation of
Funding*, Edinburgh: Scottish Executive

Scottish Executive (2001c) *For Scotland's Children: Better Integrated
Services*, Edinburgh: Scottish Executive. Available from URL
www.scotland.gov.uk/library3/education/fcsr-00.asp (accessed 1 May
2005)

Scottish Executive (2004a) *Expert Reference Group: Report on Activity
March 2003–March 2004*, Edinburgh: Scottish Executive

Scottish Executive (2004b) *Protecting Children and Young People:
Guidance on Child Protection Committees, Consultation Draft
September 2004*, Edinburgh: Scottish Executive

Scottish Executive (2004c) *Moving Forward* Additional Support for
Learning Act implementation newsletter, Issue 1, September 2004,
Edinburgh: Children in Scotland

Scottish Executive Education Department (2003) *Insight 7: Key Findings
from the National Evaluation of the New Community Schools Pilot
Programme in Scotland*, Edinburgh: SEED

Scottish Executive Health Department (2004) *Guidance on The Same as*

You? Partnership in Practice Agreements (PiPs) 2004–2007, Edinburgh: Scottish Executive

Scottish Health Promoting Schools Unit (2004) *Being Well — Doing Well: A Framework for Health Promoting in Schools*, Edinburgh: Scottish Health Promoting Schools Unit. Available fromURL www.healthpromotingschools.co.uk/files/beingwelldoingwell.pdf (accessed 1 May 2005)

Scottish Office (1998a) *Meeting the Childcare Challenge: A Childcare Strategy for Scotland*, Edinburgh: The Stationery Office

Scottish Office (1998b) *New Community Schools: The Prospectus*, Edinburgh: The Stationery Office

Scottish Office (1998c) *Shaping Scotland's Parliament*, Edinburgh: The Stationery Office

Scottish Universal Newspapers (1983/4) *The Stirling Observer*

Sharma, N. and Dowling, R. (2004) *Postcards from Home: The Experience of Disabled Children in the School Holidays*, Barkingside: Barnardos

South Ayrshire Educational Services (1999) *Developing Educational Clusters into Partnership Arrangements that Support the Development of Community Learning*, Ayr: South Ayrshire Educational Services

South Ayrshire Psychological Service (2001) *Prescat: The Way Forward Consultation Document, February 2001*, Ayr: South Ayrshire Educational Services

Stewart, A., Petch, A. and Curtice, L. (2003) 'Moving towards integrated working in health and social care in Scotland', *Journal of Interprofessional Care*, Vol. 17, No. 4, pp. 335–50

Stirling Council Playservices Homepage: www.stirling.gov.uk/index/leisure/play-homepage.htm (accessed 3 August 2004)

Strathclyde Region (1987) *Young People in Trouble*, Glasgow: Strathclyde Region

SWSI (Social Work Services Inspectorate) (1992) *Another Kind of Home: A Review of Residential Child Care*, Edinburgh: HMSO

Tett, L. (2002) *Community Education, Lifelong Learning and Social Inclusion*, Policy and Practice in Education No 4, Edinburgh: Dunedin Academic Press

Tett, L., Munn, P., Kay, H., Martin, I., Martin, J. and Ranson, S. (2001) 'Schools, community education and collaborative practice in Scotland', in Riddell and Tett (eds) (2001), pp. 105–23

Tisdall, E. K. M. (1997) *The 1995 Children (Scotland) Act: Developing Policy and Law for Scotland's Children*, Edinburgh: The Stationery Office

Wilkinson, E. (2003) *Early Childhood Education: The New Agenda*, Policy and Practice in Education No. 6, Edinburgh: Dunedin Academic Press

INDEX

Additional Support for Learning Act
  (2004) 10
adult education 2
Adult Education (Scotland)
  Regulations 2
adult services 43–4
Alcohol Concern 64
alcohol programme 22–3
Allan, J. xi, 67, 69–70
Alternatives to School Exclusion
  (HMIE) 18
attainment/social inclusion 20–1
Ayrshire, South xii, 25, 26
  see also Early Years Forum

'The Bank' project 44–5, 46
Baron, S. xi, 65, 66
behavioural difficulties 30–1
Beresford, B. 38
Better Behaviour, Better Learning
  (Scottish Executive) 18
bi-lingualism 17
Bloomer, K. x
boundaries xii, 5, 8, 9, 30, 33, 34, 43,
  51, 59, 61-3, 69, 71
British Association for Counselling and
  Psychotherapy 21
British Columbia 17–18

CALM (Consultation, Advice, Liaison
  in Moray) 55
CAMHS (Child and Adolescent Mental
  Health Services)
  NHS Scotland 54
  referral rates 49–50
  renamed 49

resources 51
  working team 48, 49
Care Commission 42–3
care/education 2, 7, 11, 42
Careers Scotland 19
Carers' Strategy, Stirling Council 41
Central Regional Council 38
Changing Children's Services Fund
  52, 59, 61
  child poverty 41
  FMC 54–5
  Playplus fund 42
  teenagers' services 43
Chartered Teacher xi, 69
Child and Adolescent Mental Health
  Services: see CAMHS
child centred/children centred 64, 71
Child Health Commissioner 54
childcare policies 5, 7
childcare working group 37
Children Act (1989) 5
Children and Young People's Cabinet
  Delivery group 8
children in need 5, 41
Children in Scotland, 2000 10
Children in Scotland, 2004 12
children/pupils 71
Children (Scotland) Act (1905) 5, 10
Children (Scotland) Act (1995) 41, 42,
  59
children's hearings system 3–4
children's panels 3
children's services xi
  FMC 53
  integration 10–11
  Kilbrandon 2–3

Play Services 40–1
Stirling Council 36, 40, 63
Circles of Friends 43
circus skills 16, 18, 64
clustering of schools xii, 26–7
Cohen, Bronwen xi, 6, 7, 58, 63–4
Coleman, P. 17
collaboration
  barriers 20
  cost effective 20
  inter-agency x, xi, 1–2, 4–5
  Playplus 61
  professionals 62, 71
  Scottish Parliament x
  support for vulnerable children
    18–21
  trust 61
community-based partnerships 48, 65
community education 2, 26
Community Health Partnerships 48
Community Planning process, Moray
  Council 53
Consultation, Advice, Liaison in
  Moray (CALM) 55
Convention on the Rights of the Child,
  UN 5, 36
crèche, council-supported 37
Curriculum Framework 27

Davies, C. 60
Department of Work and Pensions
  Extended Schools Childcare Pilot
    Scheme 8
Developing Educational Clusters,
  Ayrshire 26
development delay 30
Dewar, Donald 6
Dialogue Youth 57
Disability Discrimination Act (1995)
  41
Disability Living Allowance 33
disabled children
  acceptance 38
  isolation 37, 45–6
  play facilities 37
  Scottish Executive 41–2
  social inclusion 43
  see also Playplus (Stirling) Limited
district nursing services 3
Drumchapel New Learning
  Community 11–12

Dumbleton, Sue xii, 72
  collaboration 61, 63
  in-house training 69
  parents 65, 66–7
  play workers 65
  supported play 60

Early Education and Childcare 7
Early Years Forum xii
  additional support needs 62, 72
  Brian case study 29–30
  clusters 27, 60
  core team 28
  Mark case study 30–2
  parents 25–6, 33
  social inclusion 28
  strengths 32–4
  structure 28
Early Years policy 7, 11
education/care 2, 7, 11, 42
Education Department, Scottish
  Executive 6
Education (Scotland) Act (1872) 2
Education (Scotland) Act (1918) 2
Education (Scotland) Act (1945) 2
educational psychologist 25–6
entitlement model 11, 42
ethos of school 22
European Network of Health
  Promoting Schools 22–3
exclusion 20, 62, 64, 65
Exploring Alcohol 22–3
Extended Schools Childcare Pilot
  Scheme, Department of Work and
  Pensions 8

Families Reading Together 16
family
  learning 15, 16, 18
  respite from caring 41
  story-reading 17
family learning co-ordinator 16, 17
FMC (For Moray's Children group)
  52–4, 67
For Scotland's Children (Scottish
  Executive) xii, 52, 58, 59, 71
From Children's Services to Children's
  Spaces (Moss and Petrie) 68
Fullan, M. 14, 19, 20
fundraising 6–8, 13, 18, 36–9, 41–3,
  52, 55, 57, 59–61, 63, 69

Galbraith, Sam 6, 7
general medical practitioners 3
Giddens, Anthony 6
Glasgow
    learning communities xi, 8, 11–12
    Youth Health Promotion 22
Grampian Health Board 48
Grampian Region Health Trust 61
Grampian Regional Council 47
Greater London Council 36

head teachers 20
health 2, 8
health co-ordinators 21–2
Health Department
    Scottish Executive 44
Health Improvement Fund 50
health promoting schools 9, 21–3
health visitors 3, 29, 30
Here's Health status 24
HMIE (Her Majesty's Inspectorate of
    Education)
    Alternatives to School Exclusion 18
home-school linking 15–18, 31–2
home visitor, pre-school 30–1
Hutchison, Douglas xii, 72
    Early Years Forum 60
    exclusion 62
    expertise 65
    parents 66
    support staff 63
    training 69

Institution for the Formation of
    Character 2
Integrated Community Schools xi–xii,
    15–18
    development programme 23–4
    Home School Link Teacher 15
    parents 16, 18
    Scottish Office 13–14
    social inclusion 14, 20
    social workers 19, 64
    teachers 69
    see also New Community Schools
integration xii, 10–11, 57
inter-agency approach 58–9
    case studies 58–9
    commitment 67–8
    Moray 51
    New Community Schools 47–8

pre-school children 25–6
    training 34, 69
isolation 37, 45–6

job-shadowing 57, 69–70
joining-up 2, 6–9
    agency remits 61
    impact 9–11
    schools 11–12
    Scottish Executive 8–9
joint-agency short term funding 57
Joint Health Improvement Plan 53
juvenile justice 3

Kane, M. 36
Kilbrandon, Lord 2–3
Kilbrandon Report 3, 12
knowledge creation 71
knowledge work 70, 71

language development 29
learning communities xi, 8, 11–12
library visits 17
lifelong learning 63
local authorities 2, 4, 64
Local Community Networks 53
local developments/national policy
    59–61
Local Government etc. (Scotland) Act
    (1994) 5
lone parents 4
lunchtime club 43

MCabe, M. 27
McCulloch, K. xi, 61, 62, 63
Mackenzie, Jeannie xii, 72
    circus skills 64
    exclusion 65
    parents 66
    social workers 62
    upstreaming 59
Members of Parliament 5
Members of Scottish Parliament 5
mental health problems
    professionals 67
    stigma 49
    teachers 65
mental health services xii
    mainstreaming 54–5
    Moray Council 48–52, 54–5, 65
    training 56

Ministry for Education and Young
  People 6, 7, 8, 12
Moray 47
Moray Council
  Children's Services Plan 53
  Community Planning process 53
  funding 61
  inter-agency approach 51
  mental health services xii, 48–52,
    54–5, 65
  voluntary sector partnership 47–8
Moray Health Services 47–8
Moss, P. 59, 68–9, 71–2
mothers in employment 4
multi-agency directives, Scottish
  Executive 52
multi-agency groups 18–19

National Debate on Education, Scottish
  Executive 6–7
National Health Service reorganisation
  48
National Health Service Scotland
  report (2003) 54
national policy/local developments
  59–61
needs
  additional xii
  additional support xii, 27, 62
  individual 66
  special xii, 4, 27
  unmet 55
Neilston village 15
New Community Schools
  CAMHS 51
  collaboration 62
  funding 52, 59–60, 61
  inter-agency 47–8
  launch 6
  parents 65
  partners 52, 63, 65, 67
  see also Integrated Community
    Schools
New Deal for Disabled People 38
Nobody Ever Wants To Play With Me
  (2003 Capability Scotland) 45
nursery schools 2, 4, 24, 27, 29
nutritional guidance 9

OECD (Organisation for Economic
  Co-operation and Development) 7,

8
Operational Management Group 54
Opie, A. 70–1
Organisation for Economic
  Co-operation and Development
  (OECD) 7, 8
Owen, Robert 2

Pack report 18
paired reading 17
Pan-Grampian Trusts 48, 50
parents
  clusters of schools 28
  Early Years Forum 25–6, 33, 66
  integrated community schools 16,
    18
  lone 4
  New Community Schools 65
  Playplus 65, 66–7
  professionals 66
  self-referral 20
partnership x–xi, 59, 66–7
  agency staff/teachers 22
  community-based 48, 65
  New Community Schools 52, 63
  social inclusion 43
Partnership for Care (Scottish
  Executive) 48
partnerships
  community-based 48, 65
pedagogues 69
Penn, H. 4
Personal, Social and Health Education
  23
Petrie, P. 59, 68–9, 71–2
play
  facilities for disabled children 37
  public spaces 68
  supported 60
  see also Playplus (Stirling) Limited
play development officer 39
Play Services
  Changing Children's Services Fund
    43
  Children's Services 40–1
play workers 39, 65, 69
Playplus (Stirling) Limited 36
  'The Bank' project 44–5
  Care Commission 42–3
  care package 42
  collaboration 61

in-house training 69
legitimacy 39
management 39–40
paid staff 40
parents 65, 66–7
playscheme start 38–9
renamed 46
social services 63
see also disabled children
PLUS 46
police 3
poverty 17, 41
Pre-Fives Initiative, Strathclyde
    Regional Council 4
pre-school children
    additional needs xii, 27
    educational psychologist 25
    home visitor 30–1
    inter-agency approach 25–6
Prescat (Pre-school Community
    Assessment Team) 27, 32
Princess Royal Trust 33
professionals
    collaboration 62, 71
    mental health problems 67
    parents 66
psychological service 19–20
    see also educational psychologist
public spaces 68
pupil councils 23

referral rates 49–50, 55
reflective time 70
Renfrewshire, East 14–15
    collaboration 20
    family learning 15, 16, 18
    inequalities 15
    multi-agency groups 18–19
    Youth Counselling Service 21
    see also integrated community
        schools
Renfrewshire Association for Mental
    Health 21
respite care 41
Riddell, S. 44
Rowan Centre 49, 55, 56, 61–2

The Same as You? (Scottish Executive)
    44
Sammons, P. 63, 65
school meals 2, 9

school medical service 2
schools 3, 11–12
Scottish Childcare Strategy 1, 7
Scottish Executive xii
    Better Behaviour, Better Learning
        18
    disabled children 41–2
    Education Department 6
    For Scotland's Children xii, 52, 58,
        59, 71
    Health Department 44
    health promoting schools 21–2
    integration xii, 8, 10
    joining-up 8–9
    lifelong learning 63
    multi-agency directives 52
    National Debate on Education 6–7
    Partnership for Care 48
    poverty 41
    The Same as You? 44
    vision statement 9
Scottish Office x, 1, 7, 13–14
Scottish Parliament x
self-referral 20
service providers/service-users 67, 70
service-users
    feedback 44
    service providers 67, 70
    support hours 45
Shoppers' Crèche 38
social inclusion
    attainment 20–1
    disabled children 43
    Early Years Forum 28
    integrated community schools 14,
        20
    partnership 43
    see also exclusion
social services
    entitlement 11, 42
    local authorities 4
    Playplus 63
    universal 63–4
social skills 29
Social Work Department 19
Social Work (Scotland) Act (1968)
    3–4, 5
social workers 19, 26, 64
Special Educational Needs Auxiliary
    31
special needs xii, 4, 27

special school 27, 28
speech development 29
Stewart, G. 6
Stirling Council
    Carers' Strategy 41
    Children's Services 40, 63
    Community Services 44
    Playplus 36
The Stirling Observer 37
story-reading 17
Strathclyde Regional Council 4, 18
support hours 45
support staff 63
Sure Start initiative 7, 18, 29, 33,
    59–60
*A Survey of Childhood Disability and
    Poverty* (2003 Capability Scotland)
    45
Sweden 11

targeted services 59, 62, 63–5, 71
    see also universal services
teacher training 23
teachers 22, 65, 69
team days 49, 70
teenagers' services 43
Tett, L. 15
Third Way 6
Thornliebank Primary 15, 16–17
Tisdall, E. K. M. 4
training
    in-house 69
    inter-agency approach 34, 69
    mental health services 56

triage system 50
troublesome behaviour 64
trust 61
12.19 46
2003 Capability Scotland
    *Nobody Ever Wants To Play With
        Me* 45
    *A Survey of Childhood Disability
        and Poverty* 45

United Nations
    Convention on the Rights of the
        Child 5, 10, 36
universal services 7, 8, 11, 53, 59,
    63–5, 71
    see also targeted services
up-streaming 13, 59, 64

voluntary sector partnership 47–8
vulnerability 18–21, 64

whole child approach 1–2, 7, 12, 58,
    63
Wiles, Chris xii, 60–1, 65, 67, 69, 70,
    72
Wilkinson, E. 6, 64
Woodfarm High 20, 22–3
working with others xi, 71

Young People in Trouble 18
Youth Counselling Service 21
Youth Health Promotion 22
youth services 21, 43
Youthstart 57